An Afghan Immigrant

My Journey from Kabul to Paris to Texas

Based on Actual Life Events

Ahmad Ansari

ISBN:
ISBN-13: 978-0692868461
ISBN-10: 0692868461

Author Contact: acansari63@gmail.com

www.anafghanimmigrant.com

DEDICATION

To all hopeless and voiceless refugees who risk their lives escaping wars, persecution and destruction

To all hardworking and innocent immigrants who leave everything behind in their own homeland in pursuit of a better life in another land

CONTENTS

ACKNOWLEDGMENTS

There are many people who had great impacts on my life and many others who helped me while writing this memoir. I find it inadequate to just say a simple "thank you" to all my loved ones and friends who have done so much for me and supported me unconditionally throughout my life and during the time I wrote this book. This is the best I can do to recognize them with words for all of their acts of kindness, love and generosity.

I would like to thank my dear father (my Baaba) and my dear Mom for all of their sacrifices, support, and love to make sure I overcame all the challenges I faced. Without their help and support, I firmly believe I would not be where I am today. My grandpa (Baaba Jaan), my grandma (Bobo Jaan), my Uncle Wahed, my best friend, and my Aunt (Khala Jaan) have always been there for me in good times and bad, holding my hand to look ahead and keep a positive attitude. Thank you for everything you have done for me. I am not sure how to thank Uncle Abdul and Aunt Shameem, my heroes, for their boundless generosity and love in helping me with my treatment and hosting me in their home in El Paso, Texas while I was being treated for my leg injury. You both exemplify the greatness of humanity. Thank you from the bottom of my heart. I am highly indebted to my dear cousin Farid who spent countless nights sleeping on the hard floor of the hospitals next to my bed, helping me like a true brother. You are an amazingly selfless individual and I will never be able to return your kindness. Thank you for all you did for me. Also, I extend a big thank you to all my siblings and the rest of my family for their wholehearted love and support.

As you will learn, my family escaped repression, torture, and political persecution in Afghanistan and came to the United States as refugees. Today, when I hear some politicians demonizing Syrian and other refugees and immigrants escaping war and devastation, it is important to emphasize that refugees are not terrorists, but they are the first victims of terrorism and barbarism. When my family arrived in the United States in the mid-1980s, they were welcomed by the great people of this wonderful country. There are so many great American friends who helped and supported my family when they arrived here. I would like to mention one particular family, Mike and Karen. Mike, a businessman at that time, heard about my family through some church services and met my Baaba who did not speak English. He offered him a job that did not require too much use of the English language. After meeting my entire family, Mike and Karen became great friends of ours. In spite of a hectic and busy life style, Mike always found time to help Baaba and the rest of my family. Baaba loved Mike like a younger brother and always had a big smile on his face when he saw Mike. Mike and Karen, thank you for all you did for us. You are not only great friends, but please know that every member of my family considers you as family.

There are so many other friends who helped me by reading my draft manuscripts, providing me feedback and corrections. Thank you very much Kathy France and Dr. Al Bovik for your kindness in reading my rough draft, giving me candid feedback and allowing me to make my manuscript better.

Last but not least, my lovely wife Negah and amazing children, Eli and Noor; thank you for your love and support and for always believing in me. You are the shining stars of my universe and I do not exist without you. Thank you for your patience with me and for your continued encouragement while writing this memoir.

1 INTRODUCTION

I have always heard that we all have a book in us and, lately, I have been thinking more and more about what kind of book mine would be. Since I travel frequently for business and spend a lot of time in airport terminals, I sometimes sit in a corner of an empty gate and watch people pass by. I see many different faces and skin colors, and some wearing outfits that disclose a few clues about them. They are old and young, with many unique personal characteristics. I have thought:

If I had the opportunity to spend a few hours with one of these passengers, it would be so fascinating to learn about his or her journey through life.

I wondered if someone were watching me, would that person be interested in hearing about my life. My answer: *Maybe.* It would depend on how fascinating and interesting my life story seemed to them.

Upon further reflection, I realized that no one knows what lies behind this brown middle-aged man's face. No one knows what I have gone through and how I have dealt with my own life struggles; not any more than I know about those passing strangers.

It may be that my own naive curiosity led me to believe that some people might be interested to know more about me. Also, now that I am a father to two amazing children, for sure they would love to know more about my past and how I dealt with personal challenges throughout my life.

I finally decided to start writing about my past, mainly to leave my children, and hopefully others, some words of wisdom that no matter what life throws in their paths, they should not forget their roots and heritage, and always fight for what is right and against injustice.

In some ways, I am a typical human being, from a different part of the world, a land that most people only know by name, unfortunately, lately for many wrong reasons. I grew up in a typical family from that part of the world, went to school, and today, living in America, have a typical job, am married, have children and, therefore, in some ways, I may not be considered any different than others.

In other ways, the story of my life and what I have gone through and where I am today may be interesting because I grew up in a part of the world during a time that turmoil, conflict, war and devastation not only had a significant impact on my life but also on the entire world.

I am from a faraway land called Afghanistan, an old country with a rich history and distinctive beauty. I was born in the early 1960s and had a fairly peaceful and happy childhood that did not last long enough for me to live a "typical" or "normal" life in my own country.

I always wonder how we end up being who we are. I am sure we all think and wonder and question a number of life impacting events, such as why we are here on earth, our ethnicity, religion, the part of the world we are born in, and so many other random facts that somehow shape the person we end up becoming. I am not a psychiatrist, but I strongly believe that where we are born and the environment we grow up in during the early years of our lives have the most impact on our future lives and personalities. For me, the fact that I was born in Afghanistan and what happened in that part of the world while growing up there were the two most critical factors that defined and shaped my future. Every major event in my adventurous life links somehow to Afghanistan, an old and beautiful country with majestic mountains, beautiful lakes and ferocious rivers, a proud and diverse population from different ethnic backgrounds that managed to share this beautiful land for thousands of years.

I am attempting to describe here what happened to my beautiful homeland and its people during the past three decades. This land, Afghanistan, was once famous for its delicious fruits and people of mosaic cultures who lived in peace and harmony with one another. At other periods in our history, our people were known for their bravery against invaders and aggressors. This land contains and protects such historical treasures as the Buddhas of Bamiyan from the 4th and 5th centuries, the Minarets of Herat from the 15th century, the Blue Mosque of Mazar-i-Sharif from the 15th century, the city of Ghazni with its rich pre-Islamic Buddhist and Hindi treasures dating long before the 7th century.

I could write about hundreds of other places and monuments that represent my homeland's diversity, all of them unique and amazing. But I will just try to give a few examples of how war and destruction not only impacted my life but also my rich homeland and, more than just me, how badly the lives of my people were affected. Through telling the story of my life, I will show how the Soviet Union's invasion brought unthinkable misery and destruction to Afghanistan and to the Afghan people. For almost a decade, the Soviets massacred hundreds of thousands of Afghans and destroyed the entire country. You will also learn about the role the United States played in defeating the Soviets and then how at the end decided to abandon Afghanistan to regional powers, Iran and Pakistan. I believe that subsequent global conflicts and tragedies are linked to what happened in Afghanistan after the defeat of the Soviet Union.

When I started to write this memoir, I have to admit that I struggled. I've always wanted to tell the story of my life. I am not an author or an artist. I am not someone with a degree in English literature and, in fact, I learned proper English only after I immigrated to the United States. I knew that writing this book was going to be difficult for me, but at the same time I had this passion in me for sharing the story of my life. In some selfish ways, I am also writing this book for myself to remind me how lucky I am to have always been surrounded by people who loved me and helped me to make sure that I did not give up. I am also writing this book for my children, who were both born in America, to tell them the story of my life, my fears, my struggles, my fights, my disappointments, my ups and downs, hoping that they will learn something and not ever give up in the face of adversity. A few years ago, a well-respected American politician I prefer not to name, a key figure in a major American city, made a serious personal choice that cost him his political career. In his last formal speech, he admitted that he had made a major mistake and that he would do everything in his power to learn from that mistake. He read a very old and insightful quote:

"The greatest glory of living lies not in never falling, but in rising every time we fall."

The quote has been relied on for its fundamental truth for 2,500 years by Chinese philosopher Confucius, football coach Vince Lombardi, activist politician Nelson Mandela, Irish author Oliver Goldsmith, and transcendentalist Ralph Waldo Emerson. I add my testimony to that truth.

I have failed many times and I have fallen many more times, but I have always made an attempt to get up, dust off, and move on. We may all look at our lives as a collection of successes and failures. Again, what I hope to achieve in writing this memoir: to tell the story of my life and hope that my readers will find it interesting and unique.

In the following chapters, I have tried my best to tell the story of my life to the best of my recollection. I have changed the real names of most friends and relatives in respect for their privacy and anonymity, and I have also tried to be not too specific with exact locations while telling real life stories.

2 CHILDHOOD MEMORIES IN KABUL –
PEACEFUL YEARS

The oldest memories I have from my childhood are from trips to Hamams or public baths very similar to Turkish baths; not just any Hamams -- a Hamams for women. I remember vividly the house we lived in, a nice home in a nice neighborhood of Kabul called *"Shahre Naow,"* the New City. We lived in our maternal grandfather's home, Baaba Jaan's home. Baaba Jaan's ancestors came to Afghanistan from the Indian Kashmir. They were merchants who brought goods to Afghanistan and decided to settle in this beautiful and mountainous country that resembled Kashmir. Grandpa, Baaba Jaan, a man of small physical stature, but with very high moral values and standards, always cared for others. As a pious man, he worked with honesty and integrity to support his family. Although he had not finished high school and after completing sixth grade, he started to work in his Baaba's business. Grandpa known for his intelligence and brightness had a beautiful handwriting.

While working with his father, he also worked for a while at the Ministry of Foreign Affairs, as a civil servant (called mirza). His nature included an open, accepting mind and tolerant thinking while at the same time being religious.

My maternal grandmother, Bobo Jaan, a gracious quiet lady from Kabul had met Baaba Jaan through an arranged marriage, but they were very loving toward each other and I rarely remember seeing them argue. Bobo Jaan's face radiated peace and calmness. A gentle soul with a beautiful smile, Bobo Jaan brought happiness to everyone around her. The house we lived in, not a large home, but two families managed to live in it fairly comfortably.

We lived with our grandparents because my Baaba worked in government jobs away from the capital Kabul. My father, worked as a provincial governor. Since Baaba worked in many different regions of Afghanistan far from Kabul and traveled most of the time, my parents decided that that living with my maternal grandparents in Kabul offered us a great opportunity to get a good education as the educational system offered much more advanced curriculum than other parts of the country.

I had an older brother, Emile, and two younger sisters, Flora and Hanna. In Baaba Jaan's house, in addition to my brother, sisters, and Mom, one of my Uncles, Uncle Wahed and my Aunt, Khala Jaan lived there. An additional member of our large family, we called Uncle Hamed, one of Bobo Jaan's nephews who had lost his father at an early age and his mother had abandoned him and three of his younger brothers. Our extended family adopted the four young boys and Uncle Hamed ended up in our house. Despite a tragic and sad life, Uncle Hamed always kept a happy spirit with a friendly and vivacious personality. Baaba Jaan treated him like his own son and made sure he always felt welcomed in our house. We loved him as an Uncle and have always had fun with him. Uncle Hamed grew up to become a hardworking and responsible person, went to school and worked after school. Baaba Jaan made sure to save every penny he earned while working hard.

My Mom, hardworking, dedicated, and a smart woman took great care of us. With a strong personality, she always pushed us to do our best in school. Sometimes we viewed her as too strict, but she wanted us to avoid hanging out with kids who spent most of their time playing outside on the street and not studying. Since my Baaba had to work away from home, Baaba Jaan played the role of a father. Like Mom, Baaba Jaan with his high standards and principles had high expectations and protected us as he always felt responsible for our well-being. We enjoyed being loved and guided by Baaba Jaan and living in the same house and the large family provided us a great deal of fun.

Going back to my oldest memories from childhood, I remember vividly going to the women's public bath with Bobo Jaan, Mom, my Aunt Khala Jaan, and sisters. I must have been 4 years old and at that time. Young boys of my age were allowed to go to women's Hamam with their Moms or other female relatives. The Hamam was located a few blocks from our house. During that time, Hamams also provided a social gathering place for Afghan ladies to get together with their friends, gossip and talk about life, politics, kids, etc. The trips to the Hamam were not short; we would spend a few hours there. Before entering a hot, steamy, large space, a fairly large and cooler dressing room, allowed everyone to get ready for going inside.

The scene inside the Hamams created a unique and animated atmosphere. Once inside the steamy Hamam room, I remember the distinctive sounds, voices, crying babies, and women talking loudly. We would typically pick a space either close to some other families or friends we knew. In the front of that large room, there were two big water tanks, one with hot water and one with cold water. People would use small aluminum water containers to take water from the large tanks to wash and rinse themselves. In that steamy hot room, I always enjoyed putting cold water on myself.

Something else that I remember doing frequently: putting my hands over my ears, closing them and then quickly opening them. This game would allow me to entertain myself, somehow modulating the noise and sounds of noisy ladies and children talking, the aluminum water containers hitting the floor, babies crying or screaming, etc. As the steamy Hamam room made me very hot, I would always ask my Mom or my Aunt Khala Jaan to take me out of that steamy and hot space for a few minutes to go to the dressing room of the Hamam that provided some temporary relief from the heat. I would do that several times before we went back home.

During the 1960s, Kabul, not a very modern city by western standards, but still offered relative "modernity" compared to the rest of the country. As a constitutional monarchy, the King and his administration at the time created a moderate Islamic country based on the concept of non-alliance, freedom of religion and relative "freedom of speech". A country the size of France, it had about 14 million habitants. The majority of the people were Muslims, however about 2 million Hindus and Sikhs lived there, had the same rights as any other Afghans and were free to practice their religions. We even had a small Jewish community with a nice Synagogue not too far from where we lived.

The country had a fairly decent public educational system with a couple of major Universities. Girls were allowed to go to school and, for the most part, had the same rights as boys. As I mentioned the country enjoyed freedom of press and freedom of expression with several independent newspapers, and a major national radio station. During my childhood years, the government maintained peace and security, and while Afghanistan was not a rich country, people managed to get by.

I am told that I had a relatively happy childhood. I started school earlier than other kids. I went to a primary school located in a dusty old building about 30 minutes walk from our house. We always had a housekeeper who helped Mom and my Aunt Khala Jaan with cooking, cleaning, and other household chores. We walked to and from school every day with our housekeeper.

I have some vague memories of my first year in school:

Our assistant principal, a tall man who wore a traditional Karakul hat, always walked around the school with a wooden stick in his hands. In my class, we had about 20 to 25 students and our teacher, a nice young lady always tried her best to maintain control of the classroom. As an average student in school, I did okay and managed to complete my first year with success.

The following year, my Mom decided to transfer my brother Emile and me to a better school known for its academic program and also closer to our house. My Baaba had also graduated from that school and wanted us to transfer to this new school called Lycée Esteqlal, also a public school funded and run by the French government. Esteqlal means independence. Since the Afghan King Zaher Shah had completed his education in France, at his request, one of the French presidents had offered to build a school and help educate young Afghans.

Lycée Esteqlal had grades one through 12, and a number of French teachers and educators were teaching students scientific subjects. Starting 6th grade, all scientific subjects, such as Math, Physics, Chemistry, and Biology, were taught in French. At the end of 12th grade, students with top academic achievements were offered scholarships to study in France at French universities.

Lycée Esteqlal, located about 15 minutes walk from our house, had a rigorous and demanding academic curriculum. Students would start learning French after 6th grade, and by the time they graduated almost all students had become fluent in French. When I started 2nd grade, I became a bit more mature and still a happy kid. The first few days of school, I found two really good friends who were sitting on the same bench in class next to me. We always sat in the front row of the class and my friends names were Nadjib and Yasseen. Nadjib came from Kabul but Yasseen had been born in a Northern Province called *"Panjshir."* Yasseen's Baaba worked as a cab driver and had decided to move his family to Kabul in pursuit of a better life.

I remember Yasseen's face clearly even today; he had two missing front teeth and whenever he smiled, he would make me laugh. Yasseen had very light brown hair, green eyes with a cute Panjshiri accent when he spoke Dari, the official primary language of Afghanistan. Nadjib, the shortest of all three of us, dark black hair, dark brown eyes, had a great personality and a very fun kid to be around. Our teacher in the second grade, Ismail Khan, a tall skinny man, who rarely smiled kept us all in check. The school had two sessions, one in the morning for secondary grade students and one in the afternoon for primary grade students. We would go to school around noon until 5:00 pm. Yasseen's Baaba would bring him to school in his old Russian-made cab, a Volga sedan, and sometimes he would wait there until school started. Nadjib and I would jump in the back seat of his car and play with Yasseen. I also remember that Yasseen brought a yogurt drink with cucumbers and mint called "doogh" in a thermos. He would share his drink with Nadjib and me. Because of the cold winters and school not being heated, we always had school during summer time. Kabul had four distinct seasons and summers were hot. During summer, we all brought a thermos with water or some other drinks like doogh. I still remember Yasseen coming to school with his thermos of cold doogh and after drinking it, he would sometimes fall asleep in class. To wake him up, our teacher Ismael Khan would ask one of us to pour some cold water from our thermos on the back of his neck. Yasseen would jump up screaming and the whole class would laugh. I enjoyed going to school and as a good student I did well.

Lycée Esteqlal offered a great opportunity for both boys and girls as one of the very few mixed schools for both boys and girls until 6th grade. After 6th grade girls and boys were sent to different schools; boys would stay at Lycée Esteqlal and girls from our school would go to an all-girls school called Lycée Malalai.

Lycée Malalai, also run by the French government offered, education curriculum very similar to Lycée Esteqlal. In the 2nd grade, my parents decided to enroll my sister Flora in the same school. She did not like going to school and cried most of the time. That first week of school when she started, the assistant principal would come to my class and ask me to take Flora home because she would not stop crying in class. This whole saga created so much embarrassment for me every time I saw my sister with the assistant principal behind my class door. My Mom finally decided to keep her home for one more year and that made me happy.

Sharing my daily lunch with my best friends Nadjib and Yasseen brought a lot of joy and happiness. Our Moms would pack lunch for us and during our lunch break all three of us found a nice quiet spot and shared whatever we had for lunch. One day, my Mom had packed some meatballs (kofta) with bread for my lunch. The strong smell of kofta let my other classmates know exactly what I had for lunch that day. A couple of kids had asked me to share my lunch with them, but since I already had my lunch buddies (Yasseen and Nadjib), I said no. So Nadjib, Yasseen and I came up with a plan to run out right after the lunch break bell to find a place to hide and have our lunch without being mobbed by the other kids. Right after the bell rang for lunch break, we ran as fast as we could. We soon realized that the entire class would chase us. Once outside running, I stumbled and fell. My backpack opened up and everything in it came out, including my delicious lunch. I hurt my knees and started crying because I soon realized that my tasty lunch had gotten smothered with dirt. No one had kofta that day, as I ended up trashing my lunch. Yasseen had brought some grapes with bread and the three of us ended up sharing that.

I continued to do well in school and once I completed 6th grade, a new state of the art high school built by the French government opened. The school, truly one of the best schools in Afghanistan became an example of great education. The new great Esteqlal School located farther away than the old school kept me even more motivated to start a new chapter of my life in such a beautiful school. In addition to having state of the art labs, the school had an Olympic size swimming pool, soccer fields, volleyball and basketball courts, and a movie theatre. In order for students to continue their education in the new school, a student's grades and academic achievements were taken into account. Unfortunately, Yasseen did not make it to the new school. Only Nadjib and I met the academic requirements to continue our education at the new Lycée Esteqlal.

The last time I saw and talked to Yasseen was in the early 1970s. I am not sure where Yasseen is today and after so many years of conflicts and wars, I hope he is alive and doing well. I know a few decades have passed since that time, but I have never forgotten Yasseen's smiling face with two missing front teeth, the young happy kid who became my best friend and always made me laugh with his cute Panjshiri accent, light green eyes, and light brown hair. I am still hopeful that I will see him someday and often think about him and his family and what they might have gone through. I miss you, my dear friend, and eating meatballs is not the same without you anymore.

Nadjib and I were now in the new Esteqlal high school, but no longer in the same class. Since the high school followed the French educational curriculum, students were grouped based on their academic strengths. Nadjib with a stronger background in social sciences ended up in a class with similar students. Since I performed better in Math and Physics, the school assigned me to a more Math/Physics oriented class. I would continue to see Nadjib during recess and talk, but we both slowly made new circles of friends. At the end of 12th grade, I learned one day that the Afghan Secret Service agents had arrested Nadjib. I lost touch with him for more than two decades, not knowing whether Nadjib had made it alive in the bloody conflicts that came upon us.

My Baaba continued to work as a provincial governor in many different parts of the country, and we continued to live in the capital, Kabul. Sometimes, during our winter school breaks, we would go spend time with Baaba.

One winter when Baaba worked as a provincial governor in the western part of the country in a place called "*Anaardara*", famous for its pomegranates, Mom decided that my brother Emile and I should go and stay with my Baaba during our winter break. We were excited to see Baaba, but not too excited to leave Kabul and miss the kite-flying season, called "*goodiparan bazi.*"

During winter school breaks, most students would spend their days flying kites and what we called "fighting kites." It created a really fun activity for kids our age during winter, since we did not have any other opportunities to participate in other forms of entertainment.

But flying kites not fully allowed or approved by Mom or Grandpa Baaba Jaan always made us afraid. Such kites were flown using strings that were coated with a thin layer of a sharp paste made of ground powdered glass, glue, and some other ingredients. During kite fighting, someone with a better and sharper kite string would be able to cut the string of another flying kite.

Our family did not approve of flying kites because of the frequent fights that occurred between young boys and even adults. Also, the rooftops of the homes were the best places to fly kites and they were not the safest places as sometimes kids would fall from rooftops and get badly injured. As Mom did not want us to get into quarrels with other kids over "kite fighting" and get hurt, she would do everything she could to prevent us from participating in this activity that my brother Emile and I loved so much and for which we had a yearning. Despite always being prevented from flying kites, we both managed to find ways to participate in "*goodiparan bazi*" or kite flying. We sometimes wore large jackets to hide our "goodiparan" kites and walked funny going up the stairs. I sometimes suspected Mom and Grandpa Baaba Jaan would just pretend that they did not see us to give us a break.

Anyway, that winter when Mom and Baaba decided that my brother Emile and I should go and spend our winter break with Baaba, we both had mixed feelings; first, schools in the west of the country where Baaba worked were still in session because of the warmer climate in the west, and the possibility of both of us going to school there during our winter break did not make us happy. We were not looking forward to going to school and missing our most enjoyable time of the year -- flying kites. After a few phone calls between Mom and Baaba, our bags were packed and Baaba sent someone to accompany us to Anaardara.

The name Anaardara means the Valley of Pomegranates. The place is close to the famous and historic city of Herat bordering Iran. The road trip from Kabul to Anaardara is a long two-day trip. Emile and I reluctantly

15

left Kabul to spend three months of our winter break with Baaba. After traveling over icy cold roads, we finally arrived and were greeted by Baaba with his big smile -- we were so happy to see him and he kissed and hugged us. Baaba looked nice, a handsome, tall man with dark black hair that he neatly combed back. He had this amazing smile that made you feel happy and welcomed. A fun person, he loved to play, hunt, travel, and had friends everywhere. He possessed an extremely charismatic and charming personality, a man with a friendly and warm disposition.

Baaba's own childhood had been filled with sadness and significant challenges. He had lost his Mom at a very young age. Grandpa, my Baaba's father, married my grandmother's sister after grandma (Baaba's Mom) passed away. Baaba's maternal side were Pashtuns and I remember my Baaba telling me that his Mom did not speak Dari and only spoke Pashtu, the second official language of Afghanistan. Anyway, Baaba's step Mom was also his Aunt, and Baaba used to tell me that the reason she agreed to marry Grandpa revolved around taking care of Baaba, still a baby. Grandpa had two more kids with his second wife, a boy and a girl. Unfortunately, Grandpa's second wife, Baaba's step Mom and Aunt, also passed away at a young age. Grandpa ended up marrying for a third time. Accordingly, Baaba wound up having many more half siblings from Grandpa's third marriage. The three kids from grandpa's first two wives, Baaba, Uncle Manan and Aunt Zaiba, stayed very close to each other. In some ways, they created their own little family within the family.

Despite many challenges, Baaba graduated from the French high school Lycée Esteqlal. He worked and studied and managed to get a college degree. He developed good relationships with some powerful people involved in politics and government. The Ministry of Foreign Affairs offered him his first administrative job. Because of his hard work and dedication, his superiors recommended him to the Ministry of Interior for a better position and became an Assistant Provincial Governor. A few years later, they decided to promote him to a Provincial Governor, a job that he maintained for several years.

I don't have any memories of Uncle Manan, but I've heard a lot about him. Like Baaba, a handsome man with a great personality and the center of attention in big gatherings. Uncle Manan got married in his early 20s and had two children, a boy named Tamim and a girl named Nadjla. Unfortunately, Uncle Manan died in his late 20s from an undiagnosed illness when Tamim and Nadjla were just babies. Later in my teenage years, my cousin Tamim and I became best friends. He now lives in Germany with his wife and two daughters and we are still in touch.

Going back to that winter break we spent with Baaba in Anaardara, after a few days of arriving there, Baaba asked one of the people who worked for him to take us to the local school, so that during the day while he worked at the office, we would stay busy studying. Anaardara, a small dusty town with a warmer climate than Kabul looked boring to us. Everything looked brown during the winter. Since the town had always been famous for its pomegranates, locals found ways to preserve "*anaar*" or pomegranates in small containers made of clay mud that somehow kept the fruit fairly fresh and preserved for the winter. The place famous for a type of anar called "*anar bay dana*," or seedless anar, with unique taste made it famous all over Afghanistan. I don't remember much about the school there; all I can say is that my brother Emile and I were not happy.

Every evening, prominent people from the town came to our house for dinner. Something that I have not forgotten is a famous dish that people ate there. As in most poor countries, people do not throw away anything that could make a decent meal. In Afghanistan, the main dish always contains some type of meat and rice, when people can afford it. The typical meat that people consume is either lamb or beef. Throughout history in that part of the region, and I believe this is also the case in many other countries; people cooked and ate the head and feet of the lamb. In Afghanistan, it is called *"kala wa Pacha"*.

In Anaardara, people made a really distinctive dish from that, called *"Kala Seer Aow"* (head with garlic). It is very typical in Afghanistan to bake bread in a tandoor, a cylindrical clay or sometimes metal oven buried in the ground. The tandoor is also used for cooking in southern, central, and western Asia. I heard that there are some regions in the Caucasus where use of the tandoor is very popular. The heat for a tandoor is created by burning wood that would turn into charcoal exposing the food to live fire, hot air, convection, and smoke.

In Anaardara, after cleaning the head and legs of a lamb, they would marinate everything in a large metallic container with garlic, salt, spice and water. The covered container is then placed inside a fire burning tandoor in the ground for several hours. Typically, the cooking starts at night and after placing the metallic container inside the tandoor, the tandoor is covered with a clay cover to conserve the heat inside. The kala wa pacha would be ready for consumption in the morning.

When we were in Anaardara that winter, Baaba would get invited to some of the prominent local elders' homes for some kala seer aow in the morning. After the early Morning Prayer, a large group of guests would sit around waiting for the feast. They first washed their hands with a portable hand washer that a young boy would carry in front of each guest. After everyone had washed their hands, they would bring fresh baked bread from the same tandoor and distribute it to the guests. Then the large container of kaala seer aow would arrive and would be placed in the middle of the serving area. The steam from the food and the strong smell of garlic were everywhere. People started eating from that large container with their hands. Although I did not like that meal, I have to admit that after a couple of times, I even started to acquire a taste for kaala seer aow.

Two weeks after staying in Anaardara, my brother Emile and I started to really get bored. We missed the fun season of flying kites in Kabul and our friends. But we could do nothing to go back to Kabul and for sure we did not want to make Baaba, who seemed so happy not to be alone anymore, disappointed. Despite trying hard to be happy, we ended up being really miserable.

One evening, before Baaba came home from work, we called the local phone office and asked the telephone operator to connect us home to Kabul so we could talk to our Mom. At the time, Afghanistan did not have a robust telecommunication system. Since we were the governor's children, the telephone operator did not say no to our request and within a couple of minutes we were connected. Mom picked up the phone, and we started to tell her how much we missed everyone in Kabul and were really bored and needed to come home to Kabul. We told her that we were both miserable and did not learn anything at school. We begged her to somehow tell Baaba to send us back to Kabul.

Mom, as a smart lady, knew the game we were playing and she told us that going to school there and learning would help us to be ahead and she continued that this would be a great experience for both of us. She also said that she would talk to Baaba and ask him to find some fun activities for us so we would enjoy our stay there. Anyway, the phone call ended with us crying.

During the telephone conversion, unknown to us, the telephone operator listened to our entire conversation with Mom -- something we did not know. I believe he tried to monitor the connection to make sure the line of communication did not disconnect, or he simply just wanted to listen to our conversation. After the call ended, it appears that the telephone operator, working in a building not too far from Baaba's office, went to see my Baaba. He told Baaba about our phone call to Mom and every small detail of our conversation with her.

Around 6:00 pm, when Baaba came home, he looked sad and upset. He called us to his room. He said he heard that we had made a phone call to Kabul today. My brother Emile and I were shocked and didn't say anything. He first got really upset that we did this behind his back without talking to him first. He said he thought we were very happy to spend time with him. We didn't say a word and after a few minutes of silence in the air, he said he would arrange for us to go back to Kabul. We knew how unhappy he had become, but we managed to get what we wanted and we both hugged him and told him that we loved him very much.

The next day, Baaba found an Afghan army officer from Anaardara planning to go to Kabul. He asked him to come to our house. The officer came the next evening and Baaba asked him to take us with him to Kabul. He planned to leave Anaardara within a couple of days. Baaba started to pack our bags and tried hard not to show any sign of disappointment. I knew that Baaba was sad; for once, after a long time, he was looking forward to coming home from work and not being alone and we took that happiness away from him. I feel bad about it today, but at that age I could not wait to leave Anaardara. A couple of days later, on a dark early morning, we left with the Afghan army officer saying goodbye to Baaba. I remember he had teary eyes and tried hard to not show his sadness while we were leaving him, but I knew he wanted us to be happy. We left Anaardara in a large bus with a large crowd of people. The dusty and bumpy road from Anaardara to another larger town can only be described as long and painful.

We switched into a large truck going to Kabul. After the Afghan army officer talked to the truck driver, he agreed to take all three of us to Kabul. He barely had space for the three of us as his truck designed to transport goods did not have much room for passengers. The main road to Kabul, designed and funded by the American government, as part of the United States help and cooperation provided a straight nice asphalt path from Kabul to the west of the country.

The first night of our trip to Kabul, we arrived in an area with an extremely cold and hard-falling snow that created a thick white layer of powder covering everything and making the road slippery and extremely dangerous. The truck driver decided to install snow chains on his truck tires. He stopped the truck on the side of the road and got out of the vehicle. The snow coming down very hard with a wind gust created a very dangerous condition. The driver came back inside the truck, his head, beard and mustache all covered with icy snow. He said that installing snow chains would be very hard in this weather. There were no other cars on the road at that late hour of the night. The Afghan army officer asked him to keep driving slowly, hoping that we would arrive in a town located several miles away and there we might get some help. After a few minutes of driving in this stormy weather, the large truck's engine started making some unusual noise and then it stopped.

There we sat, late into the night and in the middle of nowhere. We did not know what to do. The driver took a flashlight outside to see what the exact problem causing the noise could be. He came back quickly and told the Afghan army officer that the radiator of the truck had been leaking and that created an ice buildup close to the leak area and it appeared that it had cracked. In his opinion the icy radiator prevented water circulation through the engine of the truck and therefore the engine had overheated.

After hearing that bad news, my brother Emile and I really got scared. The Afghan army officer and the truck driver started coming up with a plan to de-ice the radiator and see if the truck engine could be restarted. The officer took some old cardboard from the back of the truck and managed to make a small fire to heat up the radiator while the truck driver tried to start the truck. I am not a mechanic and I don't know how but after about 30 to 40 minutes, they managed to get the truck started. Emile and I could finally breathe easily now and hoped there would be no more surprises for the rest of our trip. We finally arrived at the town that was several miles away from where had been stranded.

The Afghan army officer decided that the truck did not offer a good solution for us to continue our trip and we needed to find another car or a bus that could take us to Kabul. In the early 1970s, a large number of tourists, especially hippies, traveled by road from Europe to Afghanistan, Nepal, India, and other parts of Asia. The abundance and the quality of marijuana or hashish in that part of the world had attracted them. The Afghan army officer told us that our only hope would be to catch a ride with one of the hippies. He decided that we should spend the night in that small town and wait until the morning to see what he could arrange. In the morning, a couple of German hippies arrived and stopped for a cup of hot tea where we had spent the night. The Afghan army officer with his broken English managed to communicate with the tourists, and they happily agreed to take us with them to Kabul, feeling much safer with an Afghan officer traveling with them. They were traveling in a very comfortable mini-van. The following night we finally arrived in Kabul. The weather felt very cold as the German hippies dropped us in the center of town. The Afghan army officer talked to the taxi driver and gave him our home address and we finally arrived home. Home sweet home, we took a deep sigh. Mom and

Grandpa Baaba Jaan and the rest of the family were waiting for us, and they were happy to see us back home safely.

That night, right after we arrived, Baaba Jaan called my Baaba, telling him that we had arrived. We were really tired and exhausted and we went straight to sleep. We were so glad to be back and to enjoy our winter break flying kites and having fun. Winters in Kabul were cold with lots of snow, but we were used to the season and nothing would prevent my brother Emile and me from having fun.

Emile and I were one year apart, and we were very close friends. As typical siblings, we played together most of the time and also fought sometimes, but we always managed to stay good buddies. Our house nestled close to a nice park and two movie theaters. We played soccer during spring and summer in the park and in the courtyard of our house.

Life for us seemed peaceful.

But everything was about to change disastrously in ways that no one had ever expected or dreamed.

3 END OF PEACEFUL YEARS

Until I reached the age of 10 or 11 years old, in the early 1970s, we lived in a peaceful country tolerant and accepting of others. As a kid, I always admired and enjoyed seeing military people with their uniforms and even dreamt about becoming one of them someday wearing that cool military uniform. I did not know anything about war and military conflicts. We lived a fairly privileged life; my Baaba, as a provincial governor provided a good life for the family and Grandpa Baaba Jaan, busy in his import/export business, did well. We lived in a nice part of town, in a relatively nice house. We were attending a great school, had a large and loving extended family with great friends.

Kabul, a beautiful old city had a unique charm to it and not too far from Kabul another gorgeous summer retreat town called *"Paghman"* allowed people to relax and have fun. As Kabul had four distinct seasons, summers were hot and sometimes brutal. We were fortunate enough to escape the heat during summers and go to Paghman for the milder weather.

Everyone loved Paghman for its delicious fruits, beautiful rivers and valleys. At one point one of the Afghan kings, King Amanullah had loved Paghman so much that he temporarily moved his capital from Kabul to Paghman during summer seasons. Also, wealthy and powerful families owned vacation homes there. Most summers, our family would also go to Paghman. When we went to Paghman, we usually rented a nice vacation house that we shared with another family we were close with.

The Paghman trips were always fun and enjoyable. Baaba would also take some time off from his work and join us. He loved Paghman, its weather, its fruits, rivers and spring waters. He would jokingly sometimes say that the spring water in Paghman could cure illnesses. Paghman, located about 35 to 40 minutes by car from Kabul, made it easy for us to get there. On the way to Paghman, a famous lake called "*Qargha*" with its crystal clear blue water invited people to stop for picnics and to enjoy the lake and the views. That's how we spent most summers.

During the winter season, we were off from school, because of the cold and icy weather with frequent snow storms in Kabul. Schools closed because of the high cost of heating large buildings, as central heating systems did not exist in Afghanistan.

Some winter seasons our family would move for a month or two to the east of the country because of the warmer climate there. A historical city, close to the border with Pakistan, called "*Jellalabad*," had become a winter resort town for people who could afford it. The king and many of his family members had built palatial resorts for themselves there. The trip to Jellalabad by car took about three and half to four hours from Kabul. The road would take you through mountainous narrow and dangerous passes. Because of its climate, Jellalabad provided a fertile ground for citrus fruits and the city became famous for them: different varieties of oranges, limes, lemons, grapefruits, and one very well-known fruit called "*Narenge*."

People used Narenge for sour dressing and also used it as a substitute for lime, lemon, or even vinegar.

Since my Baaba loved to travel, every year we looked forward to our trip to "*Mazar-i-Sharif*," one of the largest cities in the northern part of Afghanistan. Mazar-i-Sharif is known for the shrine of Hazrat Ali, the son-in-law of the Prophet Muhammad. According to the local legends, Hazrat Ali had told his loved ones that after his death they should place his body on a white camel to save his remains from being desecrated by his enemies. There is some belief that Hazrat Ali's remains ended up in Mazar-i-Sharif. That is why the people built a beautiful blue mosque there in the 1200s. Most other Muslims believe that Hazrat Ali's actual burial place is in Najaf in Iraq. As Afghanistan is still using a solar calendar, the beginning of the year coincides with the beginning of the spring season. To celebrate the New Year and visit the Hazrat Ali Shrine, Afghans who can afford to travel often go to Mazar-e-Sharif. My family always made sure to go to Mazar-i-Sharif every year to visit the Shrine of Hazrat Ali and to celebrate the New Year there.

The road from Kabul to Mazar-i-Sharif is precarious and dangerous. It goes through the top of the lofty Hindukush Mountains and the Salang Pass. The Salang Pass, built by the Soviet Union in the 1950s and opened in 1964, connects the northern parts of Afghanistan to Kabul, and it played a major role during the invasion of Afghanistan by the Soviets. Hundreds of poor Afghans died when building the Salang Pass due to the unsafe and dangerous work conditions.

We would typically travel by bus for the long trip, almost 10 to 12 hours from Kabul to Mazar-i-Sharif. On several occasions we experienced close encounters with danger. On one trip as the bus reached the top of the Salang Pass (always full of snow and ice, especially during that season), the bus driver decided to install snow chains on the tires to make the drive less dangerous.

Unfortunately, the inexperienced bus driver stopped the bus on a steep uphill slope to install the snow chains. The bus driver got out of the bus along with his assistant, referred to as *"the cleaner."* The cleaner had placed a small rock behind one of the rear wheels of the bus to stop the bus from rolling backwards. The load of the bus full of passengers and the steep slope of the hill along with the malfunctioning parking brake of that old bus allowed the bus to roll over the rock. The bus now without a driver kept rolling backwards.

Scared passengers started to jump out because the bus headed toward a cliff with a drop-off of more than 200 yards. People inside the bus were panicking, praying, and screaming to get out of the bus before its deadly fall. Fortunately, a heavy construction truck with a more experienced driver going uphill noticed what appeared about to happen and stopped our bus by hitting it from behind. The bus stopped when we were about 10 yards from falling off the cliff. That fall would have most certainly killed us.

On another trip to Mazar-i-Sharif, about an hour from that city, there is a famous narrow mountain pass called *"Tanguee Tashkurgan."* Due to a recent major earthquake in the northern part of Afghanistan, rocks were falling from that narrow mountain pass onto the road. The day we were going through that narrow pass, several passenger buses and cars were hit by heavy loads of falling rocks and were buried under the rocks, killing a large number of passengers. When our bus arrived at the entrance of the mountain pass, traffic police monitoring the situation inside the pass and the rate of falling rocks were signaling vehicles whether or not to risk going through the pass.

After waiting more than two hours at the entrance of the mountain pass, the traffic officers finally authorized the bus driver to quickly drive through the pass. Our bus driver decided to take the risk and with the approval of all the passengers who were praying started to drive toward the pass. The old asphalted road inside the mountain pass had become a dangerous bumpy passage full of rocks piled several stories high, burying other unlucky passenger buses and cars that drove through the mountain pass during the worst time when the earthquake had caused heavy loads of large rocks to fall on them.

Once we entered the mountain pass, we heard some smaller rocks hitting the rooftop of our bus, and the courageous bus driver did everything he could to maintain control of the bus and go through the pass as fast as he could. Once we were about to exit the pass, we heard a loud noise and everyone in the bus screamed. We thought the top of our bus had been hit by some large rock. Fortunately for us, a large rock had fallen on the front right side of the bus, flattening one of the tires. The bus driver managed to get the bus out of the pass to a safer area. Once there, he noticed that the large rock had not only damaged the tire, but had also dented a large side of the front of the bus. All of the passengers got out of the bus, as it became clear that we could no longer continue our journey on that same bus. We waited for almost three hours for another empty bus to come from Mazar-i-Sharif and take all the passengers there.

My Baaba had a couple cousins who lived in an old and famous city of "*Tashkurgan*," not too far from Mazar-i-Sharif. One of Baaba's uncles from his mother's side, a businessman trading goods between the different regions of Afghanistan lived there. In one of his business trips to Tashkurgan, he had decided to marry a local woman from Tashkurgan and lived there until he died. During some of our trips to Mazr-i-Sharif, we would stop in Tashkurgan and stay with Baaba's cousins for a few days. Tashkurgan is another Afghan city also famous for its pomegranates. Tashkugan has a long history as a stop on the Silk Road and major

28

businessmen with their large caravans enjoyed some rest and great food before continuing to their destinations.

Baaba enjoyed hunting. On one of our trips to Mazar-i-Sharif, he decided to take some time off and leave early, taking me and Emile with him on a hunting trip to "*Samangan,*" which is another province in the north on our way to Mazar-i-Sharif. Emile and I were very young and not much into hunting, but we enjoyed traveling with Baaba as he made these trips really fun. A week before the rest of the family, Baaba, Emile and I left Kabul with all of his hunting gears for Samangan, where he knew a fairly rich and powerful landowner, Haji Jora Baay who also owned a large number of "*Buzkashi*" horses.

Buzkashi is a sport that is mainly practiced in Central Asia and for a long time had been the national sport of Afghanistan. In Buzkashi, horse-mounted players attempt to place a goat carcass in a circular goal and whichever team managed to reach the highest score, won the game. It is a rough sport that requires significant strength and very strong horses. There is an old and famous movie "The Horsemen," starring Omar Sharif, based on a book by a French author, Joseph Kessel that is about Buzkashi and the horsemen who practiced that sport in Afghanistan.

During that hunting trip, after arriving in Samangan, Haji Jora Baay greeted us very warmly as he expected us to be his guests for the entire hunting trip. The morning after we arrived in Samangan, a large number of Haji Jora Baay's people arrived on Buzkashi horses to greet us and plan our week-long hunting trip. Baaba had recently received a new hunting shotgun from Uncle Abdul from America and couldn't wait to use it.

The plan: ride these Buzkashi horses and go into a valley known for hunting and camp there for a few days. About 20 to 25 people would go with us, all on horses. Since Emile and I had never been on a horse before, one of the local men asked me to try this beautiful, strong white Buzkashi horse. I probably had reached 11 years at that time. I felt excited and a bit nervous as he helped me into the saddle.

Within a few seconds the horse went wild and threw me up in the air like a load he did not appreciate. By the grace of God I did not get hurt but had a few scrapes and bruises on my arms and legs that I discovered the next day. Several local horsemen rushed to help me. Relieved that I looked fine, an old horseman, who also looked like a wise man, came and started talking to me. He told me that horses are very smart animals, especially Buzkashi horses. He continued that before riding a horse, you need to bond with the animal, start talking to him, letting him know who you are, feeding him, grooming him, and building trust.

He took me back to the same horse that disliked me and asked me to start petting him while gently talking to him, letting him smell me and then feeding him a little. After 10 or 15 minutes of spending time with that same horse, I started riding that horse again, scared and worried, but soon realized that the horse no longer acted wild and became much friendlier toward me this time. We finally became friends and he now trusted me. I spent the next two days with that horse and enjoyed riding horses from that day on.

Baaba enjoyed hunting with his new shotgun. We spent the nights camping under a large tent. Our hosts cooked us a nice meal using wood fire as everyone sat to warm up and chat. We stayed in that valley for two days and then decided to end our hunting trip and go back to Samangan. That hunting trip with Baaba is engraved in my mind, as we truly enjoyed our time with him and experienced different and beautiful parts of our beloved country.

As you can see, life treated us really well, but things were about to change drastically, not suddenly but slowly over the next several years.

In the spring of 1973, one night while sleeping, in the early hours of one morning we heard loud noises and explosions outside. Before that time, I had never heard the sound of an AK-47 machinegun or the sound of a tank firing. We would only see soldiers marching and tanks during Afghanistan's Independence Day and enjoyed that show. This may sound naive, but at that age I never imagined that the guns the soldiers were carrying, the tanks roaring on Independence Day, and fighter jets dancing in the blue sky were instruments of war and were made to kill people. That spring morning of 1973 became the first time I had experienced hearing the loud sounds of machineguns firing, tanks on the streets, and fighter jets in the sky.

We all went to the courtyard. Grandpa Baaba Jaan looked worried but tried to reassure us that everything would be fine, but we noticed that with every loud noise how concerned and uncomfortable he become. Uncle Hamed and Uncle Wahed were talking to each other and one of them said this could be a coup d'état. I did not know what that meant. At that time, Afghanistan did not have television stations; we had radio as our only form of entertainment and receiving news updates. The only government-run radio station operated during the day. While hearing all the sounds and activities outside, we did not go out of the house and around six o'clock in the morning we heard some revolutionary and military music on the national radio. A few minutes after that, some general from the Army read a statement that "*Sardar*" (meaning Prince) Daoud Khan, King Zaher Shah's cousin, had taken over control of the country and would soon speak to the nation. About an hour later, Daoud Khan, with a very loud and distinctive voice, came on the radio and announced that he had taken charge of the country and Afghanistan would no longer be a monarchy. He abolished the monarchy and declared himself the first President of Afghanistan, taking the power from his cousin, King Zaher Shah.

During this coup, King Zaher Shah had gone on a trip to Italy for some medical reasons and Daoud Khan took advantage of his absence to take over the country. My uncles were happy to hear the news that the country would no longer be ruled by a king and they were hoping that Afghanistan would soon become a true democracy, and that people would be able to vote and select their representatives and future presidents.

Grandpa Baaba Jaan still worried about the uncertainties and what might happen next seemed uncertain about the future. Thinking about that event now, it is amazing how someone within a few hours can take over an entire country. Anyway, that bloodless military coup allowed Daoud Khan to be firmly in control of the country. The king decided not to come back from Europe and start a civil war and accepted Daoud Khan as the new ruler and the president of the country. Daoud Khan allowed all members of the royal family to leave Afghanistan and join the king in Italy. What seemed even more fascinating is that Daoud Khan's wife was the deposed king's sister. But I guess when it comes to power, sometimes family relationships do not matter that much.

During the king's reign, Zaher Shah had allowed some form of political freedom. Afghanistan had a "free" press and also a number of political parties were allowed to exist as long as they did not create too much of a headache for the king. There were two leftist parties with strong ties to the old Soviet Union. It is now known that Daoud Khan had befriended many of the leaders of the Afghan Communist Party. In his first cabinet, he appointed some of the leftists to some important key positions. He also started to build closer relationships with the Soviet Union.

Life for us did not change that much as, instead of a king, we now had a president who came into power through a military coup. Daoud Khan tried to introduce some modest reforms to the country and tried to make some insignificant changes. Under Daoud Khan, my Baaba no longer worked as a provincial governor; instead, he took another administrative position at the Ministry of Interior, but still worked in many different provinces away from home. He would come home more often, as his new responsibilities allowed him more flexibility.

I continued going to the same school, and in 6th grade we started learning French. My first French teacher, a typical French lady showed extra kindness in teaching us a new language. A short and petite lady with very light blonde hair and blue eyes seemed caring and enjoyed teaching us. None of us in the class spoke French at that time. The first day communicating with us became a challenge and one could write a nice comedy about that day and how we started to learn French for the first time. Our French teacher in one of her first actions decided to learn our names and also to teach us the French alphabet. Over the next couple of days, after learning how to correctly spell our names, she gave each one of us a piece of paper with our first and last name written on it. She would ask everyone to loudly pronounce our names and after repeating it many times, she would try to make some additional corrections on that piece of paper. After spending several minutes with each one of us, she managed to spell and pronounce our names correctly. I believe this "major" accomplishment gave her a lot of satisfaction, knowing, spelling and pronouncing all of our names correctly. After that day, we slowly started to learn French. I really admired her patience with us and she clearly showed how good of a teacher she was. If we did well on our exams, she would always give us a reward. The rewards mostly consisted of items she either had received from her friends from France or items she had purchased herself and brought with her from France.

One of my first rewards from her, an Eiffel Tower postcard that one of her friends had sent her showed me how beautiful that man-made metallic tower that rose so high to the sky of Paris was. I really loved that postcard and always stared at its marvel and beauty, this beautiful tall, perfectly symmetrical metallic tower in the center of Paris representing a great symbol for its people. Some days I would daydream about going to Paris and climbing the Eiffel Tower. I continued to do well in school and learned more difficult and challenging new things. Most scientific subjects were going to be taught in French by the French teachers. The academic curriculum in our school had been designed based on the same French program, books and system used in French schools and offered us a chance to acquire a great education.

Mom always made an attempt to push us to do better in school; she had hired a private tutor who would come to our home after school and work with us. During that time, my elder uncle, Uncle Abdul, completed his education at the Kabul University Medical School and my youngest Uncle Wahed started college studying Civil Engineering at the Kabul's Polytechnic University. Mom had big dreams for us to become highly educated, either a doctor or an engineer. Uncle Abdul finished his medical residency and officially became a practicing physician. His compassionate and caring nature made him a great doctor. I don't remember him living with us, as I think by the time we were born, he had moved out of the house to go to college. I believe he lived in a dorm throughout his college years.

During the time he studied at the medical school, he had met his future wife. At that time and even now, arranged marriages are more common than young people dating or falling in love before getting married. Uncle Abdul met his future wife, a student at the Kabul University's Medical School while studying there. The government encouraged young men and women to pursue college education together at the universities. Uncle Abdul ended up marrying her and not following the tradition of arranged marriages. We called Uncle Abdul's wife Aunt Shameem. A quiet lady, she had a great personality. She acted gentle and always kind to all of us.

A few years after they got married, Uncle Abdul passed a rigorous medical test administered by the Americans, as the United States in need of more medical doctors allowed capable foreign medical doctors to immigrate the United States; therefore, they administered a rigorous medical test for doctors from foreign countries and if they passed the test, they were allowed to move to the United States.

At that time, Uncle Abdul and Aunt Shameem had three little children, two girls and a boy. I must have been in 8th or 9th grade when they left Afghanistan and moved to the United States. In the United States, Uncle Abdul completed his residency in anesthesiology and started to practice as a medical doctor.

Life went on: school, friends, sports and family kept us busy and happy. One period during the year that we really had fun was during the month of Ramadan, or the Muslim month of fasting. Muslims fast during that month from sunrise to sunset, do not drink or eat during the day. Since we lived in a fairly large family, we always looked forward to the dinnertime during Ramadan. Everyone would gather around the "*Destarkhwan*," a large piece of cloth on the floor with dinner dishes neatly arranged on top of it.

We always had guests for the entire month of Ramadan. Our housemaids, along with the ladies, would prepare all types of dishes for "*Iftar*" or breaking fast. We lived a few blocks from a large mosque, and we could hear the evening call to prayer signaling the end of the fasting period and time for the evening prayer. This is another one of the most joyous memories I have. In our house, we had a large stone terrace facing our courtyard. When Ramadan happened during summer, after dinner, we would all go and sit on the terrace and have tea, fruits, and other desserts.

Adults talked about everything from politics to weather and other current events while looking at the blue sky full of bright stars.

Another ritual during the month of Ramadan took place in the middle of the night. People fasting during the day would wake up before sunrise and eat. We called it *"sahar."* As kids we really enjoyed waking up with the adults who were fasting the next day. Since kids were not fasting and going to the school, most of the time, they would not always wake us up. Anyway, we all enjoyed the month of Ramadan as it brought changes to everyone's daily habits and then at the end of Ramadan, the *"Eid"* festivities began. Families and friends would visit each other. Kids received gifts or money from adults.

In 1978, when I was 15, our family got larger, as Mom gave birth to twins, my youngest brother and sister. I felt really excited to have a baby brother and a baby sister. They were named Abe and Mina. I was in 10th grade at school and life couldn't be more exciting for me. Becoming more fluent in French, I enjoyed going to school and also playing sports, especially soccer. My brother Emile and I would go to the park across from our house and play soccer with other neighborhood kids. We also studied hard. As Mom wanted us to excel in school, she had hired another private tutor for us -- a teacher at our school. Right after school, we would rush home to make sure we arrived on time for our private tutoring sessions. He worked with us for an hour or two. We always tried to finish our homework before doing anything else. The country still peaceful allowed everyone to have a decent and normal life. We still enjoyed our summertime in Paghman and winters in Jellalabad.

Yes, for the five years since the bloodless coup of 1973 life had kept its normal peaceful pace. Then in the spring of 1978 what happened not only affected my family, it also started the beginning of a nightmare that impacted the region and the rest of the world.

4 WAR AND DESTRUCTION - THE BEGINNING OF A NIGHTMARE

The spring in Kabul is one the best seasons. After a cold winter, plants and trees begin to become alive again. The warmer weather invites migrating birds to add even more beauty and liveliness to this old and beautiful city.

The spring of 1978, not different from any other spring seasons, transformed the beautiful city's look once again.

My parents had bought both my brother Emile and I brand new bicycles. We enjoyed the bike rides to and from school. Our school rides took about 25 to 30 minutes by bike. As teenagers, we would go to school, play sports, and have fun with a few selected friends and the rest of the family. We weren't particularly interested in politics. Except for that bloodless coup five years ago, we had not seen or experienced wars or major military conflicts, and never worried about the future.

President Daoud Khan, who initially had allied with the Afghan Communist Party and also became a close partner of the Soviet Union, had suddenly wanted to cut ties with his ex-allies. He started a policy of rapprochement with the West, the United States and such countries as Saudi Arabia. He started to imprison some prominent Afghan communist leaders, and made several trips to the West and Saudi Arabia. All of these policy changes were happening during the height of the Cold War. Looking at the history of Afghanistan, its geography and physical location have always prompted regional powers, international superpowers and empires to invade Afghanistan. Over time the Mongols, Alexander the Great, Great Britain, the Soviet Union and a few others have tried to invade and conquer Afghanistan.

Because of its rugged and mountainous terrain and its extremely proud and independent minded people, no invader had succeeded. The Soviet Union feared that President Daoud Khan, by jailing the key Afghan communist leaders and with his new pro-Western policies, may have decided to create an anti-Soviet, pro-American government on the Soviet southern borders. Since the Soviet Union had already been providing ideological and financial support to the Afghan communists, key Soviet leaders started to become extremely worried and felt they had to take action. Some of the high ranking Afghan military leaders were educated in the Soviet Union. In addition to their military training, they had also received ideological training, making them valuable assets for the Soviet Union.

On a beautiful April day in 1978, while attending school like any typical school day, we heard rumors about some military activities. Our French Lycée Esteqlal, nestled adjacent to the Presidential Palace, allowed us to hear and sometimes see major activities around the Presidential Palace. Around 10 or 11 o'clock in the morning, we started hearing the sound of machineguns. We had no idea about the events causing the machinegun fire. During school recess, we started seeing tanks on the streets and a very unusual military presence. Rumors started to spread that President Daoud Khan wanted to arrest all Afghan communist leaders. That may have been the reason he had asked the military to maintain law and order in the capital city.

Throughout that day, we kept hearing more and louder noises and explosions but still did not know exactly the reason for these very unusual activities. School ended at the regular time in the afternoon. My brother Emile and I rode our bikes home and noticed more and more military vehicles and tanks on the streets.

When we arrived home, Grandpa Baaba Jaan looked worried but happy to see us coming home safe. My Baaba worked in the one of the provinces a few hours away from Kabul. My Aunt, grandma, Bobo Jaan and Mom were also home. Soon after we arrived, Uncle Wahed also got home, followed by Uncle Hamed.

Grandpa Baaba Jaan let us know he felt happy to see that everyone had made it home as the sounds of military tanks and other loud vehicles, as well as loud explosions, started to increase significantly. Adults in the house started to speculate on what could be happening. My Uncles would say that President Daoud Khan, as a firm and changed leader, most likely wanted to eliminate the communist influence in the country. They assumed the fighting may have been caused by some Afghan communist supporters. Grandpa Baaba Jaan made sure that no one left the house.

Around 5 o'clock in the evening, we felt that things must be escalating. Military fighter jets started to fly in the sky. But we still believed that everything would be fine and that President Daoud Khan still controlled the country and no one could dare to challenge his power and harm him. I had never before seen so many military jets in the sky. They appeared to be Russian-made fighter jets, Mig 21s.

The Soviet Union had trained the Afghan Army and also supplied military equipment and arms to Afghanistan. My uncles and I were in our courtyard watching these amazing flying jets putting on a show by swiftly changing altitudes and directions, making loud noises as they would go up and down. It was around 6 o'clock pm, while out in our courtyard watching the military planes, standing next to Uncle Wahed, that I noticed one of the fighter jets suddenly dropping altitude in a nose-dive type of a maneuver. I first thought that the fighter jet would crash into our house and the next thing I remember is a huge explosion inside our courtyard, smoke and fire lighting up. The explosion blew me away by several yards and I don't remember any pain or bleeding right after the explosion. What I distinctively remember is the smell of gunpowder, smoke and fire. The next memory I have is seeing my brother Emile rushing towards me trying to help me to get up. He pulled me up by holding me and asking me to walk. I don't recall a great deal of details about the events of that evening. All I remember is that when my brother Emile held me standing, I fell to the ground.

I did not know at that time the explosion had completely shattered my right leg. We later learned that one of the fighter jets for some unknown reason had shot several rockets into our house. Beside my severe right leg injury, I sustained many other injuries in other parts of my body. I slowly noticed heavy bleeding from the right side of my face, but I didn't feel any pain yet. Emile soon realized that I was badly injured and could not walk, so he took me in his arms and carried me over to a small room that Grandpa Baaba Jaan had fixed for Uncle Hamed. Emile laid me down on a bed there. took a piece of clothing from a closet, and tied it around my shattered right leg to stop or at least control the bleeding. Then he ran out. I went in and out of consciousness. I remember my Mom screaming, my Grandma Bobo Jaan crying from pain with a broken leg and asking someone to help her son, Uncle Wahed, who was badly injured. My Aunt Khala Jaan, my sister Hanna and Uncle Hamed were also injured. Emile, my sister Flora, Mom, and Grandpa Baaba Jaan, who were inside the house during the rocket attack, were not injured and they were running around helping the injured ones.

Emile tried to come and check on me every few minutes and trying to comfort and console me, telling me that they would transport us to a hospital soon and I needed to be brave and stay alert. I later learned that my Aunt Khala Jaan who had also sustained many injuries had gone out into the street begging bystanders to help us. With everyone being scared of what had just happened, my Aunt finally decided to stand up in front of a small Volkswagen and begged the driver to take a couple of us who were badly injured to the hospital. A nice man in that car with his wife and his young daughter, decided to help us. Since Uncle Wahed and I were the two badly injured ones, they decided to take us to the hospital first. Emile came and carried me to the back of this tiny vehicle. Again, not fully aware and conscious I noticed that they were carrying me out of the house, but once in the car I started to feel some pain in my right leg and also saw that the bleeding from the right side of my face had not stopped. Then I saw Mom and Emile bringing Uncle Wahed and placing him in the front seat of this small car. In the car, I believe, Mom sat next to me crying and praying; my Aunt Khala Jaan also sitting in the back seat moaning from the pain of her own injuries.

I don't have a clear memory on how we got to the Ali Aabad Hospital, one of the best hospitals at that time in Kabul. Affiliated with the Kabul University Medical School, the hospital provided the best possible care to patients and considered as one of the best hospitals in all of

Afghanistan. Uncle Abdul, before going to America, had worked there as a physician and my family knew a number of doctors at that hospital. I do remember arriving in front of the emergency room of the hospital. They first came and took Uncle Wahed, who had many broken bones and was bleeding heavily. Then a couple of male nurses came to take me out of the car from the back seat of that car. They had to move the seat forward and lean it to the front of the car.

Then one of them asked me to get out of the car. By that time I had some realization that my right leg had been completely shattered by the explosion as every bump on the road to the hospital caused me a sharp stabbing pain and gave me a clear indication that my right leg had been badly fractured. I remember clearly that I told the nurses that my leg is broken and it hurts badly and I can't get out of the car without some help.

But one of the nurses told me, "Come on, man, you are a big boy; be brave and get out of the car on your own or it will be more painful to pull you out of there." Despite trying hard, I could not move. Somehow, the nurses pulled me out of the car with me screaming from pain. By now the darkness of night had closed in and they laid me down on a stretcher outside of the emergency room. They started cutting my bloody and half-burned pants with a pair of scissors. Then they cut the piece of clothing that Emile had wrapped around my thigh to stop the bleeding. I have this vague picture of my Mom with a long coat full of blood stains from top to bottom going between injured family members, crying and praying. The next memory I have is two nurses carrying me into the operating room and Mom holding a small copy of the Quran on my head, telling me that God would protect me.

I do have some fuzzy memories of the operating room -- like doctors around me with their masks talking. What I remember next is the day after surgery waking up in a hospital room, at first not knowing what had happened to me. Then I noticed this large bloody cast on my right leg going up to my chest. This very heavy plaster cast made it very difficult for me to move. My jaws were tied to my head with a large piece of medical gauze wrapped around my head. My other injuries were also covered with medical gauze and tape.

There were about 7 to 8 patients in this large hospital room. Most of the patients in that room were injured during the past 24 hours. Next to me, one of the patients, a nice young man who studied at the University of Kabul tried to talk to me. One of his knees had been badly hurt during a fire fight in downtown Kabul. He said "Hi" to me and with a very kind manner introduced himself, telling me his name, Aziz. For some reason, he already knew my name. He tried to reassure me that everything would be fine. I started to realize and remember what had happened to us. I started to become afraid of asking the hospital staff if all injured members of my family were still alive. Without me asking, Aziz told me that everyone from my family made it alive and doing fine, and most likely I had the worst injuries of all but he gave me assurance that I would walk again and would fully recover. Within a few hours, I saw my Mom and Grandpa Baaba Jaan entering the room. Seeing them after what had happened made me so happy. They both kissed me and told me that my surgery went well and I would make a full recovery. I asked them about other members of the family. They told me that everyone went through their surgeries successfully and were doing fine and recovering nicely. I later learned that Uncle Wahed had lost his hearing and had several broken bones and had one of the worst injuries on his shoulder. A piece of shrapnel had entered from the front right side of his shoulder and exited from the back of his shoulder. At the hospital since they placed him on a stretcher, initially, the nurses and doctors could only see the front part of his injury where that shrapnel had entered his right shoulder and had missed the open wound on his back. He had continued to lose a large amount of blood; his blood pressure continued to go down. The doctors were giving him additional blood through his IV, but his condition continued to worsen. After a while, one of the nurses noticed a large pool of blood under his bed and after further examination they noticed the open wound in his back causing the bleeding. They finally managed to control and stop his bleeding. After a few hours, his blood pressure became stable enough to allow him to go through surgery. After surgery, they kept him in the ICU for another two days. On my third or fourth day in the hospital, they brought Uncle Wahed to my hospital room.

I believe a number of foreign friendly countries including the United States had helped build the hospital we were in. The staff and management of the hospital did a fairly good job maintaining this old medical facility. Some of the well-known physicians of Afghanistan worked at the Ali Aabaad Hospital. At that time, Afghanistan had established good educational relationships with the United States, Europe, and the Soviet Union. Highly ranked graduates of the Kabul University Medical School would receive scholarships to go abroad and acquire further training and education. Some of the doctors at the hospital had received training in the United States, France, Germany, and other developed countries. The doctor who performed the operation on Uncle Wahed studied and received training in the United States and became a well-known cardiothoracic surgeon in the hospital. I think by the time they brought Uncle Wahed into my hospital room, his condition had improved and he did not need to be in the ICU unit. But I could see that he had many serious injuries and quickly recognized that he would have a long road to recovery and his life had changed forever. He had plaster casts on his arms, his major shoulder injury was completely covered with post-surgical medical gauze wraps showing signs of blood, and he could not hear because the loud explosion damaged his hearing system completely.

By now there were about 12 to 14 injured patients in my hospital room. Some patients were placed on beds and some were lying on mattresses on the floor. Uncle Wahed arrived in my hospital room on a hospital bed, but they placed his bed in a corner of the room where I could barely see his face. He could not see me either. Heavily sedated, the hospital staff continuously gave him strong pain medications. He was not fully conscious. Every few minutes he would scream and would curse the people who struck our house with rockets for no reason.

I had mixed feelings when I saw him after that night we got injured; on one hand, happy to know that he made it alive; on the other hand, I felt so bad for him; he may have been either 27 or 28 years old, fairly recently married for over a year with a baby girl, educated as a civil engineer, and had a typical normal life before the rocket attack. Now I didn't know if he would ever hear again, use his arms and was not sure how "normal" he would be in his physical and psychological aspects. In this large hospital room, I sometimes thought I was in a nightmare -- patients everywhere were complaining from pain, crying, or asking for their relatives. Some were young teenagers, others were older people. The male and female patients at the hospital were segregated. The hospital staffs were busy but friendly. Family members who were not injured would come to visit us every day, several times a day and that provided some relief and something that I was looking forward to and that helped me stay positive.

As I mentioned, my Baaba worked in a province out of Kabul when we were injured and he had no idea of the rocket attack on our house. The day of the military coup and the following day, people could still hear gunfire and assumed that the fighting was still going on. I think by the end of the second day, it became clear that the military coup orchestrated by the

Soviet Union to support the Afghan Communist Party to take the power from Daoud Khan who they no longer trusted. Military leaders associated with the Afghan Communist Party played an instrumental role in the coup. By the end of the first day, they had managed to occupy the presidential palace, and had killed President Daoud Khan and his entire family. They started to capture and eliminate all of the high-ranking government officials. Nour Mohammad Taraki, the head of the "Khalq" or people's faction of the Afghan Communist Party became the new president of Afghanistan. The new government officials told my Baaba that he was no longer needed and terminated his job. But he lucked out -- they did not arrest or kill him. The next day Baaba took a taxi and left the province where he worked to come home to Kabul. He had no idea about what had happened to all of us.

The following is a summary of what Baaba told me when he arrived at our destroyed house and how he reacted when that taxi driver dropped him off in front of the house that we lived in: Baaba said that when he saw the devastation, he first wanted to make sure the taxi driver dropped him at the correct address. He quickly realized that a major tragedy had hit our family and the half destroyed house in front of him was our house. He noticed the completely damaged front door of our house as he entered the courtyard, his heart started to race faster and faster as he saw the extent of what had happened. Large beautiful pine trees were cut in half; our Flamingo bird lying dead in the middle of the courtyard.

The explosion had caused a fire that burnt half of the house. He saw blood everywhere, bloody shoe prints, broken glass, and large holes in the ground. He started calling names but no one responded back. The neighbors on the right side of our house were our close relatives and except for some broken windows, their house did not get any major damage. Luckily, all members of their family were safe without any injuries. The house next door belonged to Grandpa Baaba Jaan's brother and he lived there with his wife and four children. When my Baaba saw the extent of damage to our house, with blood everywhere, he told me that at first he thought we were all gone. He said he became too afraid to even ask anyone about us. He told me that he wished he came a day earlier to be with us when the rocket attack had happened. After seeing all of what had happened, he went to a corner of the courtyard as his legs gave in and fell to the ground sobbing like a child. For a moment, he didn't know what to do. He finally collected himself and went outside and knocked on our relatives' house next door.

Baaba Jaan's brother's wife we called "Qand Jaan" opened the door for Baaba and started crying once she saw him. Qand Jaan, a kind lady, tried console dad; she quickly told Baaba that everyone had survived the rocket attack and not everyone was injured. All injured members of our family were recovering at the hospital. Although a bit relieved, Baaba still felt terrified not knowing how badly we were injured. Qand Jaan also told Baaba that my younger siblings, my twin brother and sister Abe and Mina were at her house, as they were not injured and Mom needed to be at the hospital with the other members of the family who were injured. Abe and Mina were less than a year old at that time. When the rockets hit our house, they were both placed on a bed close to a large glass window. Mom told me that she first checked on them right after the explosion and noticed that they were both covered with broken glass from the window, but somehow were not injured.

Baaba went to see Abe and Mina, hugged and kissed them and thanked God to have given them a second chance to live. He then rushed to the hospital we were in. I remember very clearly when Baaba entered my hospital room -- he saw me once he opened the door and ran towards me crying and sobbing. I cried too as we hugged and kissed. He first looked at my facial and other injuries and then saw that I had a large cast up to my waist under the covers. He pulled the covers and saw the blood-stained white plaster cast and cried some more. After a couple of minutes, he collected himself and told me that I would be fine and he would do everything he could to make sure I would fully recover. He then decided to go and see Uncle Wahed, tried to hug him and talk to him and soon realized that he could not hear. I could see tears coming down his face. He then decided to go see everyone else. He left the room to see my sister Hanna, my Aunt Khala Jaan, and Grandma Bobo Jaan, who were in a different section of the hospital.

Since I could not move from my hospital bed, I could not go and see the other injured members of the family. The first few days, I suffered from pain caused by my injuries as well as the surgery and because of my face and jaw injury, it made it very difficult for me to eat or talk. My face and other smaller injuries started to heal after a few days, but I knew that my right leg severely damaged would take a very long time to heal. The uncertainty of a full recovery bothered me a lot. I had nightmares of not being able to walk again like a normal teenager and that angered and deeply saddened me at times.

The hospital provided us decent medical care and three meals a day. Because of the lower quality of the hospital food, every day my Mom would prepare food at home for all injured members of the family. She would cook our favorite dishes in our half-destroyed house. We did not have modern kitchens with natural gas or electricity. Finding fire wood for cooking created a major challenge for Mom, but she managed to take care of two young babies and also took care of all seven injured members of the family every day. During that during this time, friends and relatives would come to our home to visit. On top of all her other chores, Mom wanted to make sure that all visiting guests were well-fed.

In the hospital, I started to get bored and tired. Aziz, the University student next to me, and I talked for long hours. Born in Kabul, Aziz and his family lived in the old part of the city where traditional Afghan musicians lived. The place is known as "*Kharabat*" and is famous all over Afghanistan, as most famous Afghan singers and musicians lived there. Aziz grew up in a fairly modest family. His father, a retired civil servant, came every day, sometime twice a day to see his son. He looked older than his age, wearing an old Karakul hat, made of sheep fur. Aziz's father, a kind man always made sure to talk to me, comforting me. Aziz had one younger sister engaged to another young University student and they came to visit Aziz almost every day.

Aziz's Mom, a petite and classy old Kabuli lady, also came to see Aziz frequently, always reciting part of the Quran when visiting her son and praying for his recovery. Since Aziz did not come from a wealthy family that could afford to bring him home cooked meals every day, I always shared the food my Mom cooked at home for us. By the end of the 2nd week, I looked at Aziz as an older brother, always caring and helping me. As I could only lie on my back all day and night, Aziz sometimes would help me from his bed by extending his arm, and holding my arm so I could move to the side for a little while. I could not sleep well in the hospital, and my only good time came when someone visited me.

The surgeon, who had operated on me, a well-known and famous doctor who had received training in France, did not come to check on me for a few days. I think he received his training in general surgery, but also performed many of the orthopedic surgeries at the hospital. He also taught as a professor at the Kabul University Medical School. After a few days, he started his rounds in the mornings and sometimes had a group of medical students with him. The first day he came with about 8 to 10 medical residents and he stopped by my bed. Without even acknowledging me, he talked to the medical residents using some complicated medical terminologies.

In the bottom of my bed rested a medical chart in a folder with all of my information, including several X-rays of my right leg. He took the folder and pulled the X-rays out. Holding the X-rays up close to a window with some sunlight entering the room, he explained the severe nature of my fractures. I remember the term he used was severe right femur fracture. I noticed something very abnormal when he explained the details of my X-rays to the young residents. My fractured bones were not positioned in a straight line inside that heavy plaster cast. It appeared that they had just cleaned up the large open wound on my thigh and then slapped a heavy white cast on top of it from the bottom of my foot up to my waist, under my chest.

When I saw those X-rays, without being a medical expert, I got worried and tried to ask the surgeon why aren't my fractured bones placed in a normal straight position. The surgeon with a very authoritative voice told me, "Son, you don't know anything about medicine, so don't ask stupid questions." They left the room and I asked someone to give me my medical folder. I started to look at the X-rays again and again, getting really worried about my leg. It appeared very puzzling to me why a highly reputable doctor would cover a very large open wound with a plaster cast. Typically, a wound dressing is changed on a regular basis and the wound is cleaned to make sure it heals properly. But in my case, the heavy white plaster cast covered everything including the large wound. A large part of the white cast showed red, stained with my blood from that wound. I started talking to Aziz about my X-rays and he reassured me that the doctor knows what he is doing and I should not worry too much.

Because of the hospital's affiliation with the Kabul University Medical School as well as the main Nursing School, every day we would see large groups of medical students as well as nursing students coming to the hospital with a professor going through patients' charts and learning about patients injuries and treatments. One day a large group of young female nursing students came into our room with a nursing professor who went through each patient's charts and explained medical issues to the nursing students. Among that group of young female nursing students, a fairly tall, good-looking young woman caught Aziz's attention. I noticed that Aziz kept looking at her. When they left, Aziz, who like me could not get out of his bed, but his injuries were much less severe than mine, looked at me and said, "I hope they come back," with a sheepish smile.

A couple of days later, that same group of nursing students came into our room, and this time Aziz seemed really looking forward to seeing that student nurse again. The student nurses started with one patient and went on to the next, and by the time they got to Aziz, that girl Aziz wanted to see stood very close to Aziz's bed and said "hello" to him. They all had name tags and her tag showed the name Zarmina. I saw Aziz looking at her name tag and by now he knew what her exact name was. That seemed like a first victory. When they left, Aziz thanked them and they moved around to my bed. Zarmina moved to the other side of Aziz's bed and stood again close to Aziz's bed while their professor discussed my injuries and treatments with the young nursing students. Aziz, realizing that this as a perfect time to engage Zarmina in a conversation, started to ask her about her day, and she quickly replied that she had a relatively decent day and she felt fine and asked Aziz how he was doing. Aziz told her that he felt much better now that she had come to see him; each smiling from one to the other. Zarmina laughed and said, "Good."

I think by then Zarmina enjoyed receiving attention from this young and good-looking student and a patient at the hospital. After they left, Aziz asked me what I thought about that girl. I had so many other worries in my mind that I only smiled back at Aziz and said nothing. Aziz, despite his knee injuries, kept a really positive attitude. Unlike me, he could sit on his bed and tried to exercise daily on his bed. He looked forward to getting back on his feet and completing his engineering degree, finding a good job to help his parents, getting married and starting a family.

A couple of days later Zarmina came to see us. I believe she actually came to see Aziz, but she told us that she came to visit two of her favorite patients. She did not wear her nursing uniform that evening and looked tall and beautiful. I think she must have been very close to Aziz's age. She had long hair, wearing a small headscarf and a long dress. She talked to Aziz for a while as I pretended to be very tired so Aziz could have a one-on-one conversation with her. As they were talking very close to my bed, I could hear all of their conversations. She lived in another part of Kabul and hoped to graduate in a couple of years and work at that hospital. After a few minutes, she asked both of us if we needed anything and we both said no and thanked her. Before she left, Aziz told her that he hoped to see her again soon. She smiled and said, "I don't know."

When she left, Aziz looked very happy and in heaven; he talked to me for an hour telling me how beautiful and nice Zarmina looked and I could see that Aziz had developed a huge crush on her. The next day, when Aziz's Baaba came in the morning, Aziz told his Baaba about this nice nursing student who appeared very caring and came every day to help us. He used the word "us." I smiled and told Aziz's Baaba that the nice young woman comes every day to see Aziz. His Baaba laughed and jokingly said to Aziz that the hospital would most likely discharge him with a wife. We all laughed.

We did not see Zarmina for a few days but finally she showed up with another group of nursing students. When she came closer to Aziz and said "Hi," Aziz smiled and greeted her. He told her that he missed her and felt happy to see her. Zarmina asked Aziz if everything felt okay with him. Aziz replied that he could not sleep well at nights. Zamia told Aziz that he should talk to his doctor to see if he could prescribe some sleeping medication. Aziz told her that he didn't feel sure that sleeping medications could help him. Aziz and Zarmina's subtle hints to each other about liking each other were very amusing to me. By now, with certainty I knew that Aziz had started to have feelings for this nursing student who he did not know very well.

Following that day, Zarmina would come and visit Aziz almost every day and they would talk for a long time. In our large hospital room, all the other patients started to tease Aziz and called him "a man in love" and everyone wanted a wedding ceremony in the hospital before Aziz's discharge. One day, when Aziz'a family, his Mom and Baaba and sister were there to visit, Zarmina came to see Aziz. As she did not expect to see Aziz's family, she became a bit uncomfortable, but started to say "Hi" to everyone and kissed Aziz's Mom and Baaba's hands as a sign of respect. She stayed for a couple of minutes and then left. I had a feeling that Aziz would someday marry Zarmina, but again, I had many other things in my mind and had more worries about myself at that time.

About a month or so later, they decided to discharge me from the hospital. With happiness I could not wait to go home. Aziz would also be discharged. By now, he managed to walk with the help of his crutches. I said good bye to my hospital buddy and wished him luck. He wrote his address on a piece of paper and I gave him our home address.

I could not walk or even sit properly in bed. The heavy weight of the cast created another major problem for me, making it very difficult for me to move in bed. Mom had prepared a nice bed for me at home. I slept in my parents' very comfortable bed. They managed to transport and carry me home to my new bed. The hospital requested that I should go back for a checkup after two months and they would remove the cast. Again, we did not know much about the large muscle injury under my cast since we could not see it as the plaster cast covered it. As an active teenager, life in bed felt very difficult, but I had no other options.

I believe after a month, all injured family members had been released from the hospital, but everyone needed care at home and Mom became the main caregiver for all of us. When we went home from the hospital, one of Baaba's maternal aunts came to stay at our house for several days to help. Baaba's aunt, this petite old classy, calm, soft–spoken and sweet lady took care of all of us and worked hard every day. She would spend hours massaging my legs and my back to prevent bed sores and talking to me. She had these petite hands and when massaging my feet would try to go inside my cast and massage the bottom part of my foot.

Grandpa Baaba Jaan had already started to fix the house, replace the broken windows, rebuild the damaged part of the house, and indeed the house looked almost back to the way it had been before the rocket attacks. We never found out why they had attacked our house. When Baaba asked someone from the new government why they attacked our house with rockets, we never heard a clear answer; sometimes they would say the pilot may have made a mistake. Other times they would say the rockets missed the target and we were just unlucky. No one really apologized for the rocket attacks. I remember one government official even getting upset because we kept asking that question about the rocket attack.

His reply still makes me laugh to this day:

"In a revolution people always get hurt" -- meaning that their military coup should be considered as a revolution and we should not even question why we were hurt, as in his words people get hurt during revolutions.

After a couple of weeks at home, I started to develop a very high fever. My parents brought a doctor home. He first expressed his shock about my wound covered with a hard plaster cast. We told him that the name of head of surgery at the Ali Aabaad hospital who had performed the surgery. He did not say anything. The doctor prescribed some antibiotics. In Afghanistan, we did not have a health insurance system; outside of public hospitals, patients were responsible for all medical expenses, medication, etc. With seven people injured in the family, medical expenses were a heavy financial burden on the working adults. My Baaba took the prescription from the doctor to a pharmacy close to our house. I started the antibiotics treatment, but my situation did not improve. After a couple of days, my parents decided to take me to another hospital closer to our house. This newer and more modern hospital named after a famous Afghan personality, a prince and emir, "*Wazir Akram Khan*", a high ranking general during the British attempts to invade Afghanistan, had a fairly good reputation.

My Baaba brought a taxi to take me to the Wazir Akram Khan Hospital. They carried me to the back seat of the taxi, taking the entire back seat, as I could not sit properly because of the extended hard cast. When we arrived at the hospital's emergency room, a couple of male nurses came and took me out of the car and moved me inside on a stretcher. The emergency room doctor came and looked at me; the nurses took my temperature, and my father explained what had happened to us to the doctor and the other ER staff. They were all shocked to see the extended blood-stained hard heavy plaster cast. The emergency room doctor told us that he needed to consult with the orthopedic surgeon on call before doing anything.

After waiting for about 45 minutes, the orthopedic surgeon came to see me. He seemed fairly experienced, probably in his late 50s or early 60s, with a serious look and demeanor. He didn't come across as very friendly. Baaba explained everything to him again and he ordered the staff to cut and open the plaster cast so he could examine at my wounds.

They took me into another room, and couple of nurses started to cut the cast. After about 40 minutes, I felt free of that heavy burdensome piece of plaster. I could not look at my leg, but from the faces of the nurses I could see that something could be seriously wrong. They called the orthopedic surgeon and when he arrived, I could see the shock and disbelief in his eyes. My wound, surrounding tissues and muscles were badly infected and I needed a couple of surgeries to first remove the infected tissues and muscles and then the doctor explained that he needed to take some skin and tissue from my other leg to help cover the large wound to heal. For now, the first priority was to take care of the infection.

During that time, they also took me to the X-ray room to take a few X-rays of my broken bones. As I had noticed a long time ago, my broken bones were attached to each other randomly, and not in a straight line. I soon realized that I would have a difficult and long journey ahead of me, and I realized the possibility of not ever be able to walk properly again, play sports, and enjoy life like a normal, healthy person.

As I mentioned, this new and more modern hospital felt and looked cleaner. After they decided to officially admit me, they moved me into a patient room with another patient, a young man suffering from a broken back. During hard times, you always expect your immediate family members to do everything they can to help. My parents, brother and sisters, Aunts, uncles, grandparents did everything they could to take care of me. I felt and believed truly blessed to have such a loving and caring family. Another member of my extended family to whom I will always be grateful is my cousin, Farid.

Farid, the son of my Baaba's sister, who studied Engineering at the Kabul University came to visit me every day, helped me with all my needs like an older brother. When he learned about my admission to the Wazir Akbar Khan Hospital, once again, Farid would ride his bike for over an hour to come and see me. He would even spend the nights in the hospital with me, sometimes sleeping on the hard tile floor and going to the university in the morning. His help, compassion and care for others are qualities that are hard to find. I could write an entire book about Farid and can't really thank him enough for everything he did for me. Today, Farid lives in Europe with his wife and his son. Farid Jaan, I will never forget everything you have done for me during the darkest time of my life. Just saying a simple "Thank You" will never do justice to your kindness, my brother.

In the following couple of weeks after my admission at the new hospital, I went through a couple of surgeries. My wound finally healed but I ended up with significantly large scars on my right thigh and a new large scar on my left thigh. The next set of surgeries would focus more on how to fix my broken bones. The orthopedic surgeon did not come across as one of the most caring doctors I had seen, and we later learned that he wanted my parents to pay him extra money to work on me. Doctors in public hospitals would receive a salary from the government, and some of them would look to patients to supplement their pay with some additional money. During one of my surgeries, once they moved me to the operating table, I saw the nurses and doctors bringing a large number of sharp surgical instruments close to the operating table. The orthopedic surgeon with his mouth and nose in a surgical mask moved closer to the operating table and I got really scared and started crying. For some reason, I thought that they would not administer any anesthesia before my surgery. While crying, I asked the orthopedic surgeon if they were going to administer anesthesia. Without a response, he slapped me on the face, telling me to be quiet. I have never forgotten that moment of sheer weakness, lying powerless on a surgery table, being slapped by the doctor for asking a question because of the horror story I had heard of patients operated without proper anesthesia medication.

In any case, they did give me some anesthesia medicine, and I went through the surgery that day. After several weeks, the orthopedic surgeon could not help straighten my broken bones. The even tried to insert a very thin metallic rod inside of my knee bones, lifting my leg on a platform and attaching heavy weights at the end of a mechanical system using strings, but without any success. I will never forget the day the nurses inserted the rod through my knee bone. My cousin Farid came to visit me at the hospital that day. Two nurses came into my room with a surgical drill. They first explained what they were going to do. I naively believed that they would first use some type of an injection to numb my leg or apply some type of a local anesthesia, but they soon crashed my optimism.

They asked Farid to stay outside of the room. They told me to pull the bed sheets over my face and if I felt pain, I should start biting on the sheets. They did not apply anything to make the procedure less painful and inserted that rod into my knee bone with me crying and screaming from pain. When Farid came back in the room, he asked me how they did it, and when I explained exactly how they did it, he expressed his displeasure and became upset. The hospital did not offer any pain medication, so Farid went to a local pharmacy outside and bought some over the counter pain medication for me that day. This whole procedure ended up being useless, as my broken bones had already been firmly attached to each other in a random way. The only way to have straightened my leg would have been to fracture it again.

I stayed in that hospital for another couple of weeks. Nothing really happened. One good outcome of going to the hospital I enjoyed that I no longer had that heavy plaster cast on me. I soon realized how badly handicapped I had become and my dreams for the future were shattered. My right leg, not straight, had severe scars, and had become several inches shorter than my left leg. Now I could walk with crutches and that gave me some sort of a freedom. Beside the physical damage to my body at that age, the psychological and emotional impacts were just as bad. Depression slowly took over and I ended up in this really dark place. Thoughts of suicide crossed my mind but the love of my family would pull me back. I also knew that taking my own life would cause even more pain and suffering to my poor parents. My family always told me that they would find a solution and help me walk again like a normal healthy teenager.

During this time my older uncle, Uncle Abdul, who had left several years before to the United States to practice medicine received the news from Grandpa Baaba Jaan about what had happened to us. The main form of communication between Afghanistan and the United States were written letters through postal services. Grandpa Baaba Jaan, worried that Uncle Abdul could possibly hear about the rocket attack on our house through other friends or family members, wanted to reassure him that no one had died and all injured members of the family were recovering. In his letter to Uncle Abdul, Baaba Jaan indicated that my Uncle Wahed had lost his hearing in both ears and my right leg had been injured severely and doctors and hospitals in Afghanistan were not equipped to provide any more help for the two of us.

Uncle Abdul and Aunt Shameem, already known for their kindness and compassion, had now four young children of their own. He was an anesthesiologist in El Paso, Texas. Within a couple of days of receiving the letter from Grandpa Baaba Jaan, Uncle Abdul sent a telegram to Baaba Jaan stating that they should do everything to get passports and visas for Uncle Wahed and me and send us to the United States for medical treatment. He also mentioned that he would personally pay for all of our medical, travel, and other expenses. In the middle of my hopelessness and darkness, this telegram from Uncle Abdul gave me hope and courage to be optimistic again.

Obtaining passport for us now became the first big obstacle. Then acquiring visas for the United States also proved to be very difficult because of the political situation. After the Soviet-backed military coup in Afghanistan, the Afghan Communist Party had formed a pro-Soviet puppet government. Throughout history, Afghans have always shown their pride in not being ruled by any foreign power. This time, for very clear and obvious reasons, the Soviets ruled Afghanistan through a puppet government and the Afghan people were about to start another struggle to fight a major superpower. The Afghan communist government started to imprison anyone they believed presented a threat to the regime. Prisons soon started to fill with educated Afghans opposing the government or simply not supporting the communists.

The government's Secret Service arrested, tortured and killed thousands of poor ordinary Afghans who did not support the new regime. People started to leave the country to escape being arrested or being killed by the ruthless communist government. Afghans with some money and means to leave legally tried to obtain passports and left the country, mainly to Germany, and to some lesser extent to other Western European countries. Millions of other poor Afghans walked for days with their families, including young children and even babies, to escape the oppression. They went on foot through the eastern and southern borders to Pakistan, or through the western borders to Iran. Within a couple of years, there were millions of Afghan refugees living in camps close to the borders with Pakistan and Iran. Slowly but surely, a military resistance movement against the Soviet-supported government started to take shape nationwide.

Under these extremely unfavorable political conditions, we started to tackle the first major challenge, obtaining passports to travel to the United States and receiving the medical treatment we needed. The government made it difficult for ordinary Afghans to leave, realizing that Afghan people applying for passports were not Afghan tourists wanting to go on vacation. They were treated as Afghan traitors not supporting the communist regime. Grandpa Baaba Jaan and Baaba, started the process of acquiring passports for Uncle Wahed and me. The first couple of passport applications were automatically rejected, as the communist government wanted to make sure that our real goal was not to escape the country.

For Uncle Wahed, it proved easier to obtain a passport since his wife and young daughter would stay behind and that fact provided the communist government some type of assurance that he would come back, as he would most likely not abandon his wife and his child. After some more negotiations with the passport office, they agreed to issue Uncle Wahed a passport. But the communist Afghan officials now running the passport office, who in the past spoke so strongly against bribery and corruption during king's rule, wanted to be bribed before they could issue Uncle Wahed a passport. Grandpa Baaba Jaan, for sure not a rich man, had to work hard to find some money from his meager savings and borrow some from his small business to bribe the communist officials to finally obtain a passport for Uncle Wahed.

For me, acquiring a passport became significantly more difficult. As a young unmarried man who did not own properties or any investment in Afghanistan to prove to the Afghan communist government that I would for sure come back after my medical treatment, my chances of obtaining a passport were very slim. The passport office kept rejecting my repeated applications for a passport. That's when we began an incredible journey through the bowels of the medical establishment -- a journey I shall never forget.

Many years ago, my Baaba had temporarily worked in the passport office at the Ministry of Interior, before becoming a Provincial Governor. He still knew some folks in that office, although the communist government had replaced all high-ranking officials everywhere in the administration. Baaba, through one of his old contacts at the passport office, found a communist official who could possibly be convinced to help. He suggested that I should obtain a detailed medical recommendation from a prominent orthopedic Afghan surgeon, stating clearly that Afghanistan did not have the medical means to treat my handicapped leg. He emphasized that the letter had to be very clear and concise, stating exactly what he asked for.

Uncle Wahed had a friend who knew the president of the Wazir Akbar Khan Hospital and after talking to him, he agreed to accompany me to the Hospital to see if he could help. Uncle Wahed's friend, an engineer like him named Zemarai, had completed his education in the Soviet Union. While a student in the Soviet Union, Zemarai had met the president of the Wazir Akbar Khan Hospital, a die-hard communist who now worked as a fairly powerful government official. They were merely acquaintances, as Zemarai himself did not have any ties with the Afghan Communist Party. Zemarai hoped that this high-ranking member of the Communist Party would help. When Zemarai took me to the Wazir Akbar Khan Hospital, we decided to go straight to the office of the president of the hospital.

Once in his office, the president of the hospital recognized Zemarai and greeted us fairly warmly. Zemarai explained why we were there, what had happened to me and that we needed his help. The president, knowing that Zemarai had no communist ties and not a communist comrade, just someone he had met several years ago in the

Soviet Union, did not offer any real help. Instead, he asked us to go see an orthopedic surgeon in his hospital, and if the doctor agreed that I could not be treated in Afghanistan, then he would give us what we needed.

I couldn't believe what happened next.

He sent us to the same orthopedic surgeon who had once slapped me on the operating table, the corrupt doctor who wanted money from patients to do anything for them. Before going to see the orthopedic surgeon, I had told Zemarai about my past dealings with that doctor. Regardless, we decided to see the orthopedic surgeon. The doctor worked in his hospital office doing some administrative tasks and when we entered his office he did recognize me. After saying hello, Zemarai explained why we were there. The surgeon started laughing and said:

"You expect me to issue a letter for him?"

He then quickly followed up and said something that crushed my hope. He said:

"His leg will stay the same way it is for the rest of his life and no one can help with that, so please leave my office as I am too busy right now."

Before leaving his office, an enraged Zemarai told him that not all orthopedic surgeons in the world are as incompetent and as inhumane as he is, and his arrogance stood as a testament to what kind of a human being he must be. Zemarai kept talking to the doctor furiously, telling him that one way or another, this young man, pointing at me, would go to America and get the proper treatment and would prove that doctors like him were a disgrace to the entire medical profession.

Once out of the orthopedic surgeon's office, Zemarai told me not to worry and that he would find another solution to help me acquire a passport. Although I did not know Zemarai that well, and he only knew my uncle, his genuineness and the fact that he really cared about helping me proved him a good man. After what happened with that orthopedic surgeon, we didn't even bother going back to the office of the hospital's president.

I came home disappointed, talking to Mom and Baaba, and we decided on another option to getting that medical letter of recommendation. We had a highly respected family friend, Dr. Nedjat who practiced at the Ali Abad Hospital, where I was taken after the rocket attack. We decided to see him and learn whether he could talk to the chief of surgery at that hospital and obtain the medical letter of recommendation. Dr. Nedjat, also worked as a professor at the Kabul University Medical School, knew the highly reputable surgeon who had operated on me the first time, the night of the rocket attack. Dr. Nedjat took Baaba and me to the office of the Ali Abad hospital's surgeon who had operated on me.

That day the Afghan surgeon happened to be meeting with a French orthopedic surgeon who came to Afghanistan for a month or two as part of a medical collaboration program. The Afghan surgeon who had poorly performed my first surgery had received some medical training in France. He spoke French fluently. When we knocked on his office door, he asked all of us to come into his office. I had my medical files along with my X-rays with me, and Dr. Nedjat explained to the surgeon what we needed. The Afghan surgeon told Dr. Nedjat that he needed to quickly consult with the French orthopedic surgeon. He explained to the French orthopedic surgeon in French what had happened to me. The French doctor took my medical files and then started to look at all of my X-rays. He showed his disbelief on how poorly the operation had been performed and conveyed his comments and displeasures to the Afghan surgeon who had actually performed that surgery on me.

All communications between the Afghan surgeon and the French orthopedic surgeon were in French. They did not know that I understood almost everything they were talking about because I'd studied French. Shamelessly, the Afghan surgeon who had done that botched surgery on my leg told the French doctor that he didn't know who had operated on this young man (me). I kept quiet during this entire exchange between the Afghan surgeon and the French doctor.

I sometimes think that the night of my surgery, this reputable Afghan surgeon who operated on me may have been overwhelmed by the large number of injured patients he had to care for, and that maybe he only tried to simply save my life quickly but did not have the time to properly treat my broken femur bones to ensure that I would not be handicapped.

After a few more minutes of conversation between the French orthopedic surgeon and the Afghan surgeon, the French doctor offered to help, but I had already lost faith in getting proper treatment in Afghan hospitals, and Dr. Nedjat kindly asked the Afghan surgeon to give us the recommendations we needed.

Reluctantly, he wrote on an official hospital paper exactly what we needed, signed it, and gave it to us. We thanked him and left the hospital, happy that now I should be able to get my passport and go to America for my medical treatment. Baaba and I went to the passport office with the letter they had asked for, certain that they would now issue my passport. Unfortunately, we still had to pay the corrupt communists at the passport office to obtain my passport. By now, Baaba knew what to do next, and after some negotiating with the passport officials, they finally agreed on a price. Since Baaba did not have enough cash, he decided to sell an old German Opel used car we had and give the cash to one of the Afghan communist passport administrators. Finally issued, my passport meant that Uncle Wahed and I had gotten one step closer to obtaining the medical help we needed.

Now we needed to obtain visas for the Unites States, not an easy task even for us. This proved to be even more difficult than obtaining passports from the Afghan government. The next morning, Grandpa Baaba Jaan and Baaba took Uncle Wahed and me to the United States Embassy in Kabul. The embassy stood in a very nice and upscale neighborhood of Kabul called Wazir Akbar Khan, not too far from our house. We took a taxi and within 10 minutes we arrived at the gates of the embassy. For security reasons, we had to walk a long way to get to the main entrance. Once we arrived there, we told the guard that we were there to apply for visas to the United States. He smiled, and now I know why. We had no chance of just walking in and getting visas.

The guard talked to someone inside the embassy using a walkie-talkie and after a thorough search, he guided us inside the main building. We were then asked to go to another section of the building for visa applications. My Baaba spoke some French and Grandpa knew some English. Behind a window, a young lady gave us two visa applications. We took the applications and with some difficulty managed to fill out the forms. We returned the visa application to the young lady and waited to be called by someone inside for an interview.

Within 5 or 10 minutes, all four of us went inside a small room. Inside that office an American diplomat greeted us. He looked young, maybe in his early 30s, very cordial and nice. He had a nice desk and after we all sat down, to our surprise, he spoke fluent Dari. He first read our applications and then asked to explain why Uncle Wahed and I were planning to go visit Uncle Abdul in El Paso. Baaba told him the entire story of what had happened to us, and he listened very carefully and with kindness. At the end Baaba told him that Uncle Abdul worked as a medical doctor in the United States and he agreed to pay for all of our expenses. We showed him the telegram Uncle Abdul had sent us several weeks ago. After listening carefully to everything we told him, he wanted to see some more documentation from Uncle Abdul, including detailed financial records, as he explained that medical treatment in the United States without health insurance would be extremely expensive. He very politely told us to write back to Uncle Abdul and ask him to send a number of additional documents, including information on his salary, bank statements, tax returns, and other financial information, and then come back.

At that Moment I quickly lost hope again, very disappointed because sending and receiving mail to and from the United States would take weeks, if not months. Also, I did not know whether or not Uncle Abdul would be able to provide all the documents required for us to receive a visa. But we had no other option but to follow the directions given to us by the embassy official. On the way home, Grandpa Baaba Jaan bought a prepaid mail envelope for sending letters to the United States. When we arrived home, Baaba Jaan started to draft a detailed letter to Uncle Abdul, explaining all the details on how we managed to get passports and then our visit to the United States Embassy. He listed all the documents the embassy needed before issuing a visa for both Uncle Wahed and me. After finishing the letter, he reread it a couple of times to make sure he did not forget anything and then went to the central post office in Kabul to mail the letter to Uncle Abdul to the United States.

During this time, both Uncle Wahed and I were still struggling and recovering from our injuries. I was able to walk short distances with crutches, as my right leg had become much shorter than my left leg and also not straight. Uncle Wahed had issues with his shoulder and right arm and still could not hear. I started going into another cycle of depression. With so many unanswered questions in my mind, the uncertainty of not ever being able to walk again like a normal healthy person, not sure if we would be able to leave for the United States, and not sure that even if we managed to go to the United States, they would be able to help me – all of these questions took me back to those dark places again.

Not being able to go to school for an extended period because of my injuries created another major issue for me personally. Since the rocket attack, I could not attend school and during almost four months in hospitals or at home recovering I missed school. That long absence from school bothered me. It appeared that I would most likely have to repeat 11th grade if I ever went back to school again.

Since the task of walking became a major problem for me, one day my Baaba took me to a local shoemaker he knew to see if could make me a customized pair of shoes to at least allow me to move or walk without crutches. The shoemaker told Baaba the only help he could give would be to create a customized pair of shoes to compensate for the length difference between my legs. He took some measurements, my Baaba negotiated the cost and he told us that it would take about a week for him to get the shoes ready.

A week later Baaba brought this burgundy-colored shiny pair of shoes from the shoemaker. One looked normal and the one for my right foot looked very awkwardly -- big and heavy with a much higher heel. I didn't like them, as I thought they were pretty ugly, but I had no choice. I tried them on to see if they could help me with my walking. The shoemaker had told Baaba that it would take me a while and some practice for me to get used to them and that I needed to start wearing them every day, walking and trying to maintain my balance. I have always had good coordination. With some practice and patience, after a couple of days, I managed to walk with these new shoes without crutches. In some ways, it became my first victory as I could walk very short distances without crutches. But I knew that even with these shoes, my walking looked awkward and funny and I could not walk for a long time, as I would get tired very quickly. As a teenager, worried about my image and that people outside may laugh at me bothered me too. In any case, now I at least had an option to walk or move without crutches.

During this time, every day, we were waiting for the mail to arrive and to see if Uncle Abdul was able to send all the documents needed for us to receive visas. I had good days and bad days, but managed to go through every day with the help, support, and love of every member of my family. They all tried very hard to show a positive attitude and were reassuring me that someday soon I would be able to recover completely.

Grandpa Baaba Jaan had a rental property attached to our house. He typically rented that property to foreigners working in Kabul, as they were much more reliable to pay rent on time and maintain his house. At that time, a German man lived in his rental house. By the way, the rocket attack had not damaged other homes around us, and except for the broken glass windows, the rental property stood unharmed. Baaba Jaan had already done all the repairs needed. The German man's name was Heinz. Heinz, a heavy man with a thick brown beard, very friendly spoke fluent Dari. He lived by himself and had a maid that cooked and cleaned the house for him.

We didn't really know exactly what job Heinz had in Afghanistan. He was not a diplomat but he claimed being involved in some type of an import-export business. Some people said that he may have been a spy, but I never believed that. Heinz knew that there were several of us injured during that rocket attack and would regularly ask Baaba Jaan about us and how we were doing. In Kabul, the western diplomats typically lived in the same area of Wazir Akbar Khan, close to the embassies and knew each other. Heinz would also get invited to some gatherings and parties hosted by the other foreign diplomats, as would other foreign visitors.

Unknown to us, Heinz had many good American friends who worked at the American embassy in Kabul. During a casual conversation with Baaba Jaan, he told Heinz that Uncle Wahed had lost his hearing and my right leg severely handicapped needed more treatment that could not be done in Afghanistan. Baaba Jaan told Heinz about Uncle Abdul in America and his offer to help us. He also explained to Heinz how we managed to bribe an Afghan communist official at the passport office to acquire passports for the two of us, but now we were somewhat at an impasse getting visas for the United States.

When Heinz heard about all the hardships we had endured for the past several months, he told Baaba Jaan that the next morning he would take us to the United States Embassy and see if he could help us get visas. Baaba Jaan came home that night and told us to be ready in the morning, as Heinz would go with us to the American embassy. I became happy hopeful again that we might now have another option of getting visas quickly. I couldn't wait for that night to end and didn't sleep much in anticipation of what could happen next.

In the morning, I wore my nice clothes along with my new awkward and shiny burgundy shoes. Around 9:00 am Uncle Wahed and I went to see Heinz. He asked his maid for a cab. Within a few minutes, a taxi showed up behind his door and all three of us were on our way to the American embassy. Once we arrived at the embassy, Heinz, who was fluent in English, told the American guard something in English, and he let us inside the compound. After a quick search, we went to the visa section of the embassy. Heinz asked for our passports and we gave them to him. He asked us to wait in a waiting area. He went inside some offices and within 30 minutes came out, meeting us in the same waiting area. He told us in Dari:

"You both now have visas and can plan your trip to the United States."

He opened the passport page that showed us the visa stamps for 3 months of stay in the Unites States. I could not believe the miracle that had just happened and we both thanked him for his kindness. He was happy to have helped us and we quickly got out of the embassy. Heinz had to go somewhere else in Kabul for business and Uncle Wahed and I grabbed another taxi to go home.

Finally a great day for me -- I had hope again and now we were finally able to travel to the United States and hopefully receive the treatment we badly needed. When we arrived home, we told everyone about how Heinz had helped to get us visas. The family felt extremely happy, hugging and kissing us. Baaba Jaan said that he would now go and send a telegraph to Uncle Abdul to start making travel arrangements for both if us. Uncle Wahed and I were finally embarking on another chapter of our lives.

A couple of days before our trip to America, we received a card in the mail, a wedding invitation to Aziz and Zarmina's wedding. I felt truly happy for them and unfortunately could not make it to their wedding. Today, I don't know where Aziz and Zarmina are, but I hope they are still happily married with lots of children living somewhere safe.

5 FIRST TRIP TO AMERICA – EL PASO, TEXAS

Within a few days after Baaba Jaan sent a telegraph to Uncle Abdul to tell him that Uncle Wahed and I were ready to travel to America, a return message arrived from Uncle Abdul with all the details of our travel itinerary.

My excitement accelerated almost beyond control. Not only would this be my first time flying on an airplane, but it also rekindled my hope for a successful treatment of my crippled leg.

Our flight out of Kabul scheduled for the first week of October finally became a reality. We would fly from Kabul to London, spend the night in London, and then leave the next day on an American airline for New York. Because Uncle Wahed knew some English but could not hear and I could communicate fairly well in French, we both thought that together we could take care of everything during our journey to America. Again, neither of us had been out of the country before and this would be our first trip abroad, so we felt some nervousness that we tried to hide. Uncle Wahed had a friend who knew London fairly well, as he had studied and lived there for several years. His friend gave us some tips on where to spend the night, how to get to downtown London from the airport, how to navigate the subway system, etc.

Uncle Abdul would take care of all of our expenses, including airfare, medical treatment, recovery, etc. Uncle Abdul and his wife both truly wanted to help us and we were very grateful for their generosity and kindness. Baaba still wanted to make sure I had some money with me while traveling. The weakness of Afghan currency against the American dollar did not help us much financially. I think one dollar equaled 50 Afghanis at that time. Baaba managed to give me $500 just in case of an emergency during our trip. That $500 represented a significant sum of money for Baaba, especially at that time, since he was no longer working.

On a sunny October morning, Uncle Wahed and I left Kabul on an Ariana (Afghan airline) flight for London. All members of the family accompanied us to the airport. I was both excited and anxious. By that time I had enough practice with my customized shoes to walk without crutches and tried hard to keep my balance. We said our goodbyes to everyone. My Mom cried when she hugged me and whispered in my ear that everything would go well and I would be fine. Uncle Wahed's wife also cried and I felt really bad for her. She was a very nice lady with a young baby girl and a badly injured husband who could not hear.

We finally went through passport control and walked into the airport toward the stair to the airplane. We both waved back to our loved ones a few times before boarding the plane. We had a smooth and uneventful flight to London and arrived in the evening. Of course, I felt excited the entire trip – my first ride in an airplane. We had already received transit visas for England for the night we were spending in London. We went through immigration without any problems. Since we had not been out of the country before, in this first trip to London we did not know exactly how to recover our luggage. We got lost in this large airport temporarily but eventually somehow managed to find our luggage. I couldn't walk properly and Uncle Wahed could not hear and had major problems with one of his injured arms. But we managed to grab our heavy bags and plan our next move.

We went to a corner of the airport and read some notes Uncle Wahed had taken when talking to his friend who lived in London. We had to buy subway tickets from the airport and then go to a specific location in downtown London called King's Crossing, where there were lots of hotels and restaurants. We made our way to the airport subway-train station where a large subway map on a wall helped us locate King's Crossing station. We felt good. We now had to buy subway tickets to King's Crossing station. We already had some money in the local English currency. Somehow, using some of my French and some of Uncle Wahed's English, we managed to buy two tickets from the airport to King's Crossing. Since we had never been on a subway before, we both were overwhelmed by the complexity of this new form of transportation. By accident, we took the right train and managed to arrive at King's Crossing.

With some difficulty, we climbed out of the subway station and emerged into the dark night into a typical light rain for which London is famous. We both started to look for a hotel. We saw a narrow street with a number of hotel signs and tried the first one. A nice elderly lady worked at the front desk of the hotel and she welcomed us. We had memorized some useful phrases in English and told her:

"We need a hotel for one night."

She had a room available and we paid with cash. She showed us our room and also said something about breakfast that we did not understand.

After about 30 minutes, Uncle Wahed said:

"Time to go eat something now."

By now we both were ready to eat something. We only had one major problem: we were not familiar with the types of food, menu items in restaurants, etc. that people would eat in London, or anywhere else outside of Afghanistan. We knew fries (as Afghans referred to them as chips) and hamburger as the only Western meals. With our extremely limited knowledge of the food selection, we ventured out and entered our first London restaurant. The place seemed nice and clean, but far from being too fancy. A nice waitress seated us and brought us the menu. That's when the problem started. We did not know anything about the food items listed on the menu and what to order and eat. She brought us water and then asked what we wanted to eat. We tried to tell her that we wanted some hamburger with chips, something we could not see on the menu. After a few minutes of trying to help us, she finally decided to get some help.

She brought the restaurant cook to our table. He was an Indian man. The cook started to talk to us in Urdu and Hindi but we could not understand it. We kept saying, "hamburger and chips." I believe the way we pronounced hamburger and chips wasn't very clear and may have butchered the words. In any case, the cook talked to the waitress, but I'm not sure what they said. The waitress took the menus from us, smiled and left. We weren't sure what would happen next. About 20 minutes later, we saw the waitress with a couple of dishes with rice and chicken and a basket of bread. We were really happy to finally eat something. We finished our dinner and decided not to go anywhere else, as we did not want to get lost in this busy, beautiful city. We were also very tired. We went back to our hotel and tried to sleep. Our flight from London to New York was scheduled the next day in the afternoon. We only slept for a few hours that night.

We woke up early in the morning. After taking a shower and getting dressed, I tried to tell Uncle Wahed that last night the old lady at the hotel had said something about breakfast. Although my Uncle could not hear, we had developed a communications system using hand gestures and lip reading that allowed me to talk to him. Uncle Wahed asked loudly since he could not hear if they might give us breakfast here at the hotel. I said:

"Maybe."

We went to the lobby and the old lady saw us, smiled, and said:

"Breakfast?"

"Yes," I replied.

She asked us to follow her and we went into a small room with a few tables and chairs. She invited us to have a seat. No other hotel guests were there yet. Our typical breakfast in Afghanistan consisted of bread, cheese, warm milk, butter, eggs, and sweet hot tea with cardamom. Again, we were not familiar with what they would eat for breakfast in England. Within a couple of minutes, the old lady brought us two bowls of cereal along with a small milk container. We had never seen cereal before and did not know what it was. Since Uncle Wahed was making some gesture asking me what the bowls contained. I had no idea. After a few minutes of looking at the bowls, Uncle Wahed said, "Chips," and we tried to eat the corn flakes cereal like chips, picking a piece at a time. They surely didn't taste like chips. We did not realize the old lady had been watching us. She thought we did not like the cereal and came back to take the bowls of cereal with her. She then brought us some tea with toast, butter, and jam. We were happy to see some bread with butter and tea.

After breakfast, we decided to leave for the airport early, as we did not want to miss our next flight to New York. We packed everything and checked out of the hotel, went to the same subway station, and bought two tickets for the airport.

One thing that we did not understand at that time: each subway line had two trains going in opposite directions. We did not know that. We were standing on a subway platform with our heavy luggage waiting for the train to take us to the airport. The train coming to the subway platform we were standing on transported the passengers to the opposite side of the airport. We had no clue.

We noticed the platform getting really crowded with more people coming and the platform on the opposite side of where we were standing with not too many people on it. Uncle Wahed said to me that we should go and try the other side as this side felt too crowded. At the time, we didn't realize that by moving to the other side we were making the correct decision. The train on the opposite side actually went to the airport. We managed to get our luggage to the other side and took the correct train toward the airport -- just by accident. Someone from above must have been watching over us because we clearly did not know what we were doing, but we finally arrived at the airport.

The airport wasn't too busy and we were really early for our flight. We checked in for our flight to New York. They looked at our passports and visas and assigned us seats on the plane. We were ready to board the airplane for America. Our flight from London to New York's John F. Kennedy (JFK) Airport placed us on board a major American airline at that time called Pan Am (Pan American World Airways). The huge plane, a jumbo jet Boeing 747, could carry 416 passengers in three classes. Once we boarded the plane, I felt as if I were already halfway to America.

Almost everything on this journey became a first-time experience for us. Flying in this jumbo jet 747 Pan Am airplane proved to be amazing. They offered us great meals and beverages and we really enjoyed a smooth flight to our destination. About 8 or 9 hours later, we landed at the famous JFK airport. Before landing, the flight attendants had given us some immigration and customs forms to fill out. We did our best to fill out as much as we could and walked out of the airplane with our forms and passports in hand.

Our next stop: the immigration checkpoint. We soon realized by looking at people, that American citizens were going through a faster lane and all others with foreign passports were waiting in a different lane. There were several immigration officers sitting in small glass-topped booths. We finally reached the front of the line and were next in line to talk to the immigration officer. He made a gesture toward us, inviting us to come see him. He very politely asked for our passports and immigration forms. We gave him all the documents we had in our hands. He started going through our passports first and saw that we had a valid visa for entry to the United States. He then looked at our half-filled immigration forms and started asking some questions. Because Uncle Wahed couldn't hear and I didn't speak English, I asked him if he spoke French.

He replied "un petit peu," meaning a little bit. He asked us why we were visiting the United States and the purpose of our visit. I somehow communicated that question to Uncle Wahed, telling him what the officer asked. As I mentioned, we had memorized some prepared English sentences in case we ran into problems. Without any hesitation, Uncle Wahed told him:

"We are sick."

The puzzled officer asked the same question again:

"What is the purpose of your visit to the United States?"

Again, Uncle Wahed replied:

"We are sick."

The officer smiled and tried to make sense of what we were saying. He did not know anything about our background and what we had gone through, unaware of the fact that we were injured during a rocket attack in Kabul, unaware that my Uncle could not hear since that day. Unfortunately, we could not communicate well enough to tell him the whole story. After a couple of minutes, he took all of our documents and asked us to follow him to a small office.

He called a lady who spoke Iranian Farsi (a language close to the Dari language we spoke). The Iranian lady asked us a number of questions and we told her the entire story, including the fact that our Uncle Abdul, a medical doctor in El Paso, Texas, waited for us to help us with our medical treatment. After about 20 minutes, the officer stamped our passports for legally entering the United States and wished us good luck.

In retrospect, this whole episode now sounds like a comedy that we often joke and laugh about.

But we were at last officially inside the United States. Our next goal: find the location of our luggage. By now almost all the other passengers from our flight were gone and we could not follow anyone who would guide us to the luggage area for our flight. We got lost in this vast airport and finally decided to show our boarding pass to someone who worked at the airport and who kindly walked with us to the luggage area. We found our bags and noticed that some people were using luggage carts to transport their belongings. We found an empty luggage cart and loaded our bags on top of it and started following some other passengers who were exiting the international arrival terminal.

The time now hovered close to noon in New York. I knew by now the sun had set by a couple of hours in Kabul. Uncle Abdul had asked two of his good friends who lived in New Jersey to meet us at JFK to help us with whatever we might need. But we didn't know how to find them and also weren't sure if they would be able to recognize us. We passed the United States Customs checkpoint without any problem. After passing through Customs, we should have taken our luggage off the luggage cart and walked to the outside of the terminal area with our bags. We did not know that we were not allowed to take the luggage cart outside of the international terminal. Since we had finally found a more comfortable way of carrying our heavy bags, we decided to take that cart with us to our next domestic flight at another terminal. The international terminal purposefully designed with a barrier to not allow luggage carts to be taken out of that area, but we found a solution; Uncle Wahed and I took our luggage off the luggage cart first and then I moved it to the opposite side (exit side) of the barrier and carried the empty luggage cart over the barrier. We then took our bags and reloaded them on top of the cart.

We were slowly walking out of the international terminal, getting close to a large automatic door, when we heard people shouting at us. Two airport employees were running toward us, not happy, and wondering why we took the luggage cart with us. We did not understand why they were so upset with us about what we had done. Anyway, they took the luggage cart from us and we took our bags and slowly walked out of the international terminal.

Outside, there were people waiting for their loved ones to come out, and we started to look around to see if we could identify Uncle Abdul's friends who were waiting for us. We suddenly saw a couple of men waving at us. I guess the way we were walking and how confused we looked gave them the assurance that we were the two guests they were expecting. They approached us and introduced themselves, helped us with our bags, and told us that we needed to change terminals for our next flight from JFK to El Paso. Our next flight scheduled for later in the evening from a different part of the airport required us to walk to another building.

We had more than enough time and now we felt much more relaxed because we had people who knew the country, food, culture, language and everything else that we had been struggling with. Uncle Abdul's friends took us to a place inside the airport to eat lunch. They first explained the menu to us and then ordered food. We ate a nice lunch and started talking to them, asking questions about America and New York. They were in their mid-30s and worked as medical doctors and did really well. They loved America and enjoyed living here. Then they started asking us questions about Afghanistan and what had happened there. We told them everything -- the savagery of the Soviet Union and how ruthless and corrupt the Afghan communists were. We told them about the imprisonment of hundreds of thousands of innocent Afghans who opposed the communist regime and told them about the random killings and assassination of prominent Afghan politicians who had decided not to collaborate with the communist regime. We also shared with them that the Afghan resistance movement spreading across the country to fight the puppet communist regime supported by the Soviet Union. After lunch and talking for a couple of hours, they took us to the domestic terminal. Our flight to El Paso had a stop in Dallas. It was an American Airlines flight. We checked our luggage, obtained boarding passes and went to our gate, saying goodbyes to our friends. We finally boarded a plane for our first leg of the flight to Dallas. When we arrived in Dallas we managed to find our gate for our final flight to El Paso. We landed in El Paso around 9:30 pm local time.

Uncle Abdul had left Afghanistan almost 10 years ago, but I still remembered his curly black hair. When we got out of the airplane, I first saw Uncle Abdul and then his lovely wife waving at us from a distance. We slowly walked toward them; we hugged and kissed, overjoyed that we had arrived. Uncle Abdul and his wife were very nice and reassured us that they planned everything for us to receive the best medical care possible and that we would be back to normal in a matter of weeks. We picked up our bags and they drove us home. I still remember their beautiful house in a nice neighborhood of El Paso. We arrived in front of their garage door and magically the garage door opened. I had no idea how advanced America had become. Wireless garage door opener remotes and all of these new pieces of technology looked like magic to us. Once we arrived at the house, Uncle Abdul picked up the phone and called a number to send a telegraph to Grandpa Baaba Jaan in Kabul, letting him know that we had arrived safely. Uncle Abdul and his wife had four kids, two girls and two boys. When we arrived home, the kids were sleeping, and Zak, the younger boy, woke up and came in the living room. About one or two years old, with dark curly black hair, he looked like Uncle Abdul. Uncle Wahed and I were exhausted. Uncle Abdul's wife, Aunt Shameem, had prepared a room for both us with two nice beds and with our own bathroom. She took us to our room and showed us everything. Uncle Abdul told us to sleep well as tomorrow we both would have a long day visiting with the doctors and medical professionals to come up with treatment plans. As we were exhausted from our long two-day trip, Uncle Wahed and I went to sleep quickly. I slept well that night and woke up in the morning peeking through one of the windows of our room to get a glance at the outside. My first morning in America, I watched the sun rose on a beautiful October day in Texas.

Soon after, we got dressed and went into the kitchen where we found all the kids, Uncle Abdul and Aunt Shameem. We said "Hi" to everyone and were happy to see my Uncle's family. The older kids were getting ready to go to school. Aunt Shameem made us a nice healthy breakfast and we were ready to start our first day. Uncle Abdul took me and Uncle Wahed in his car and drove us to the hospital where he worked. Uncle Abdul had already made plans for me to be admitted at the hospital he worked in and had consulted with an orthopedic surgeon who worked in that hospital about my treatment.

People at the hospital were very nice and friendly. After some paperwork, a nurse took me to my hospital room. Uncle Abdul left me there because he needed to take Uncle Wahed to another medical clinic that specialized in treating ear injuries and hearing. After an hour in my room, a doctor came in and introduced himself as Dr. Zeloud and I believe he was born in Czechoslovakia. Like Uncle Abdul he had immigrated to the United States to practice medicine. He was an orthopedic surgeon and started examining my right leg. He continuously talked to his assistant who took notes. After about 30 to 40 minutes, they left and I could not understand a word they said. Soon after, a hospital nurse showed up and took me to the X-ray room. The X-ray technician had a note from Dr. Zeloud and took a number of X-rays. Before lunch, a couple of nurses came into my room to take my blood for more lab testing.

After lunch, around 2:00 pm, Uncle Abdul came back with Dr. Zeloud. Dr. Zeloud had all my X-rays with him and they started talking. Dr. Zeloud clipped each X-ray to a lighted white screen on the wall of the hospital room and explained different aspects of my injuries to Uncle Abdul. I still didn't know what they were going to do. Finally, Dr. Zeloud left the room and Uncle Abdul started talking to me. He told me that I would need at least two surgeries. Dr. Zeloud would first operate on my leg to break all the bones that were not connected to one another in a straight normal way, and then using an orthopedic procedure he would attach weights to a system that would allow my leg to rest on it. They would also insert a metallic rod into the top part of my knee, similar to what they had done in Afghanistan. The hope was that after a couple of weeks, the weights would stretch my thigh enough to allow all the broken bones to align, and then once my right injured leg reached the same length as my left leg, Dr. Zeloud would proceed with another surgery, using a titanium plate and screws to attach all the broken bones in my thigh together. I felt more than ready to go through the surgeries.

They scheduled my first surgery for the next day, very early in the morning. I remember seeing Uncle Abdul in the operating room with Dr. Zeloud. The first surgery went well and several hours later, I woke up in my room attached to a system with my right leg elevated and weights hanging from my knee. I felt some pain, but the nurses took great care of me. Uncle Abdul had written a number of useful sentences in English on a piece of paper with translations in Dari, in case I needed something to show the nurses to help me communicate when he was not there.

Every day, they would measure the length of my right leg to see how much it had stretched. Unfortunately, my muscles were really tight and even with all broken femur bones and significantly more weights, my leg had not stretched. I started to get worried. Uncle Abdul and his wife were visiting on a daily basis and doing their best to keep my spirits up. After almost a week and no progress, Uncle Abdul came to my room one day and talked to me. He said:

"Unfortunately, what they had originally planned did not work; they are exploring another option."

Since he himself was an anesthesiologist, he explained that one of the side effects of local anesthesia is to relax muscles and tissues. He planned to administer some local anesthesia medication through the lower back of my spine, numbing the lower part of my body for a few hours and see if that would help stretch my leg. Within an hour he came back with two nurses and asked me to sit on my bed. I was scared about the idea of a needle going into my spine. I saw a fairly large syringe in Uncle Abdul's hands and with the two nurses holding my arms Uncle Abdul started the process of injecting the anesthesia medication into my lower back. Within a couple of minutes, I could not feel the bottom part of my body. The nurses injected some pain medication into my IV system. Everyone left the room and I went to sleep. The next morning Uncle Abdul came in early in the morning, checking on me. He had a measuring tape with him and he started to measure my right leg and could not believe what he saw. All I could see was a big smile on his face. He hugged me and said:

"We did it!"

My leg had stretched enough for Dr. Zeloud to proceed with the second operation, inserting the titanium plate and screws to align my bones. I shed tears of joy for one of the happiest days of my life.

Without delay, Dr. Zeloud scheduled my next surgery for the following day. My second surgery went well and I had a long titanium plate with seven screws inside my thigh, holding all my broken bones together and aligned. The day after my second surgery, Dr. Zeloud came into my room with Uncle Abdul. He felt happy about the outcome of the surgery. I did not have a heavy plaster cast and Dr. Zeloud asked me to stand up and use crutches to walk without putting any weight on my right leg for at least a month. I still felt some pain, but nothing now would stop me from standing.

They gave me some crutches, and within a couple of minutes I stood up and slowly started walking. For first time in a long time, I had hope and felt truly excited about the future. Uncle Abdul could not stop smiling at me. I went straight to him and hugged him. I regarded him as more than an uncle and like a second father who truly cared about me. The doctors and the hospital decided to discharge me the following day.

During the time I was in the hospital in El Paso, Uncle Wahed underwent treatment in another specialized clinic for ear injuries and hearing. He went through a couple of microscopic operations by ear surgeons who tried to reconstruct the inner parts of his ears that had been damaged or destroyed by the loud explosions. Uncle Wahed and I got reunited at the house. He slowly regained his hearing by wearing a hearing aid. The doctor had told him that he would not be able to fully recover, but with the help of some type of a hearing aid he would slowly be able to hear again.

We were both nicely recovering at Uncle Abdul's house. We enjoyed playing with my cousins. Outside, they had a swimming pool in the backyard and a basketball court. It felt too cold to swim but nice enough to play basketball. We kept ourselves busy and after about two months, Uncle Abdul planned a road trip from El Paso to Las Vegas. They had a Volkswagen minivan designed in an RV style with a small table and chairs as well as a small refrigerator inside. It had enough room for all of us. I still used crutches to move around.

Uncle Abdul possessed a really fun and jovial personality. He loved sports, playing games, going to the movies, traveling, and vacations. On an early morning in mid-December, we left El Paso for our road trip to visit Las Vegas. Our first road trip in America and a fun one -- we traveled through the Arizona deserts, passing through some amazing scenery. The kids were singing in the van, laughing, playing cards and other games. We stopped somewhere in the middle of the desert in Arizona, and I got out of the van still walking with my crutches. Uncle Abdul looked at me and said:

"I think it has been more than a month since your last surgery, and you should start carefully walking without your crutches."

That did it. Once I heard that, I took both of my crutches and threw them as far as I could. I slowly and very carefully walked back to the van. I was free at last -- no more crutches. Because of significant muscle loss on my right thigh, I still could not walk without a limp. But I felt happy to be able to walk again and walk without any assistance. The trip to Las Vegas took us two days, and we arrived there at night. Once our van entered the Las Vegas Boulevard, I thought we were in a different world filled with amazing buildings covered with colorful flashing lights and people everywhere.

Uncle Abdul had reserved rooms for all of us in a nice hotel on the strip. Being too young to walk on the casino floors, I could only hear the sound of the coin machines and some occasional screaming from lucky winners. Uncle Abdul liked to play poker and I believe he did play some, but he spent most of his time with us walking on the strip, eating good food, and having fun. On our way back to El Paso, we took a round-about-route and went through San Diego because one of Uncle Abdul's best friends lived there. He was a physician, too, and invited us for dinner at his house. We only spent one day in San Diego before driving back to El Paso. Our ten-day vacation had been a marvelous experience.

Our flight back to Kabul had been scheduled for the end of December. Uncle Wahed wanted to go back to Kabul to his wife and daughter as he missed them dearly. I also missed the family back home, my Mom and Baaba, my brother Emile and my two sisters, including the twins, Baaba Jaan, Bobo Jaan and my Aunt Khala Jaan. Uncle Abdul and Aunt Shameem talked to me about staying with them and not going back. They wanted to enroll me in school there because of all the unrest, fighting and insecurity back home. They tried to convince me to stay with them. I had really become close to both of my uncles, but going through a rough year together with Uncle Wahed, we had become very close friends, roommates and travel buddies. Despite our age difference, he became my best friend, my confidant, and I did not want to let him go back home alone. I decided to go back to Kabul with him. The day finally came for us to say our goodbyes to Uncle Abdul, his wife, and children. We thanked them profusely for everything that they had done for us and especially for me. I would never be able to repay them and I am eternally grateful to them. This is my message to them:

"Your acts of generosity, kindness, and love will never be forgotten, Uncle Abdul and Aunt Shameem. You have not only helped heal my injuries, you have also changed me as a person. You made me a more compassionate and caring person and you gave me hope and another reason to live. I only wish there were more people like you in this world. Thank you from the bottom of my heart."

On our flight back to Kabul, we stopped in New Jersey to spend some time with Uncle Abdul's friends and in-laws. They were also physicians and extremely nice and hospitable folks. We visited New York City, the Statue of Liberty, the Empire State Building and other famous landmarks. New York is typically very cold in the month of December. Our flight back to Kabul had a stop in Frankfurt, Germany. Going back, we were much more at ease. We now spoke some English and were physically and mentally stronger. We were ready for the next chapters of our lives. After spending a night in Germany, we finally arrived in Kabul in the middle of the winter season. We were both happy to see everyone and they were happy to see us.

Looking back, that year I spent in the hospitals, going through major surgeries and dealing with so many ups and downs made me a stronger person. I also had a different outlook on life. I wanted to do well and become a successful person in life and help others. A couple of days after my arrival in Kabul, I wanted to re-enroll myself back at the French high school and I set a goal to do everything I can to earn a French Government Scholarship through the school and get a good education in France after high school. Every year, the French high school would award a few scholarships to the top students of the graduating class to go to France and study at French universities. The entire scholarship program was managed by the French Embassy in Kabul and funded by the French government. I wanted to start a new chapter of my life and felt that after all the hardships

I had gone through I finally was in charge of my own destiny. With determination, I was eager to restart school and do really well.

6 BACK TO KABUL – FINISHING HIGH SCHOOL AND SCHOLARSHIP TO FRANCE

For me to go back to my French high school, Lycée Esteqlal, after a long absence, I had to get special approval and permission from the Ministry of Education. Since I had not gone on a year-long vacation abroad to have fun, and because of everything that had happened to me, I thought allowing me back in my high school would be a mere formality. Only the Afghan Minister of Education, a hard-core communist, could approve my request.

Baaba made an appointment for us to see the Minister of Education. His name: Dastagueer Panjshiri. We arrived at the Ministry of Education and waited in his waiting room. After about an hour, a young man came and asked us to follow him. They first took us into a small room and searched us to make sure we were not armed and dangerous; then allowed us to enter the office of the minister. We respectfully said hello and my father explained what had happened to me. Without any kind words or an apology for the rocket attack, he started lecturing us about revolutions and workers' rights. He wanted to know why I had gone to the United

States for medical treatment and not to the Soviet Union. He didn't find our explanation satisfactory and after a few more minutes of lecturing us about becoming more patriotic, he reluctantly signed the approval for me.

We left the Ministry, unhappy about how we were treated, but relieved that I had achieved what I wanted. I took the approval letter to Lycée Esteqlal, located a couple blocks from the Ministry of Education, gave it to the assistant principal, and officially re-enrolled in 11th grade. I could not wait to restart high school again. I had this firm determination in me to do really well.

Prior to my injuries because of my academic achievements in scientific subjects, the school assigned me to 11M1, the top class for students with higher grades in math and physics. Even during the first couple of years of the communist regime, we still had a small contingent of French teachers at our French high school. A couple of years after I graduated, because of the increasing insecurity and war, the French government decided that Afghanistan had become unsafe for French teachers, and all French educators left Afghanistan. The Afghan communist regime gladly took over Lycée Esteqlal, our amazing French high school, the pride of our nation and transformed it into a Soviet-style high school.

I did really well in 11th grade. One of my very smart classmates named Kabir, who did not study as hard as I did, became one of my academic rivals. Kabir, a Pashtun from the southern part of the country, had a great mind and with outstanding problem solving abilities. Because I viewed him as my rival academically, he really pushed me to work even harder. I was ranked number one among all 11th grade students by the end of the year and Kabir finished second.

By the end of 1979, the Afghan communist regime faced more resistance from the Afghan people in every corner of the country. The regime realized that their weak and unmotivated army would not be able to protect them. The Soviet Union decided to invade Afghanistan militarily with more than 100,000 troops, backed by tanks, fighter jets, helicopters and other military equipment. The Soviets hoped to crush the Afghan resistance movement. Right after their invasion and military intervention, they also decided to remove and kill one of the Afghan communist leaders, the president of Afghanistan at that time, Hafizullah Amine, and replace him with another more trusted figure from a competing faction of the Afghan Communist Party named Babrak Karmal. They hoped the new president could be more effective.

By now the Soviet Union had officially invaded Afghanistan and had direct control of the country. A few weeks later, more civilian protests in all major cities across Afghanistan started to create additional problems for the Afghan puppet government and the Soviets. But with the inhumane brutalities and savageries that the Afghan communist government and the Soviets were known for, they started shooting at peaceful, unarmed demonstrators and protesters with live ammunition using AK-47s. Hundreds, indeed thousands, of old and young men, including teenagers, were massacred on the streets of the major cities of Afghanistan. Just in the historical city of Herat, there were estimates of more than 50,000 people killed. There were horror stories of people burying their dead loved ones in the backyards of their homes, fearing more persecutions from the government.

I also experienced a close encounter with the authorities one night during that time. For almost a week, we would receive hidden messages from anti-government groups in the capital arranging massive anti-government and anti-Soviet demonstrations. Every night, a piece of paper would be dropped behind our front door telling us to get ready to peacefully demonstrate on a specific night against all the atrocities of the communist government and the Soviet Union.

On the scheduled night, once it started to get dark, we started hearing anti-government slogans and chants from inside some homes and it quickly spread across town. A couple of hours later, it sounded as though the entire resident population of the city of Kabul chanted anti-government slogans. I decided to see what was going on outside, and without telling anyone, I went out of the house and saw a number of our neighbors and friends on the street talking. They were trying to organize a peaceful demonstration.

One of the men on our street named Wali from a prominent family lived across the street from our house. Wali stood tall, young man with a brownish French style beard, a member of the Afghan National Volleyball Men's Team, and a highly educated man who had just completed his Master's degree in Germany. He came to join us and told us that no matter what everyone had to stay together in a group, as it would make it more difficult for the regime to arrest a large group of folks than single individuals.

We slowly got organized. I had my sandals on, stayed in the back of the group. We started marching and chanting anti-communist and anti-Soviet slogans. While we were marching, we heard occasional machinegun fire, but we thought they were shooting in the air to scare people. After walking a couple of blocks, we suddenly saw a Russian-made military vehicle with its high beams, driving at a high speed toward us. The vehicle stopped a few yards in front of us and about eight or nine armed police officers came out from the back of the vehicle. The AK-47s they were holding were on their arms in a threatening position. One of the officers screamed:

"You guys need to go home quickly or we will shoot you."

I felt scared to death and thought that we would surely die right there on a street close to home. Wali, who somehow had become the de-facto leader of our pack, paraded in the front of our group. He approached the officer who threatened us. Wali wore grey traditional Afghan clothing, long shirt and a loose pair of pants. He first tried to talk to the officers, but they did not want to have a conversation with us.

Once Wali got within a couple of feet of one of the officers, he put both of his hands on the collar of his shirt and without any fear tore his shirt apart in front of the officer, exposing his chest. He told one of the officers that he is not afraid of him, and that anyone like him holding an armed AK-47 threatening peaceful demonstrators and telling them that he would kill them was not a real man. Wali continued:

"Shoot me if you are a man."

Now really scared, I thought that the situation had escalated enough for something horrible to happen. A police commander, who had been in the vehicle, came over to talk to us and told us in a calmer voice to just go home. He also stated that they were not associated with the Secret Service Police and they were from our local police district. He warned us that if we get caught by the Secret Service Police, we would all be either killed or arrested. After hearing that, I decided to run home as fast as I could, barefooted, leaving my sandals on the street.

During the next 24 hours, hundreds of young Afghan men were shot dead on the streets of Kabul. We quickly learned how lucky we were that night to go home unharmed. Several months later, we learned that Wali had been arrested by the communist Secret Service Agents, and I believe he ended up spending a few years in prison as a political prisoner.

My senior year in high school became a highly critical year for me. I felt determined to excel and earn a scholarship so I could go to France. It offered me a ticket to freedom, to escape a possible war, and avoid being arrested by the communist regime. The communists had created organizations in every school to indoctrinate and brainwash young students with their ideology. I believe that similar tactics were used in the Soviet Union, and they were forcing students to join these youth communist organizations called *"Sazman–e-Jawanan."* I did not join their organizations and some of my friends were either forced or threatened to join. The country became even more unstable during that critical senior year in high school. The Afghan resistance movement started to become stronger, supported by the West and the United States. Groups of freedom fighters called "The Mujahedin" were fighting the Afghan communist regime and the Soviets in almost every province of Afghanistan. During this time period foreign fighters from other countries also came to Afghanistan to fight the Soviet Union.

Usama Bin Laden and his followers were also fighting in Afghanistan against the Soviets, and they were supported by the United States and the West.

I continued to hope and pray that the French government would keep their staff at our high school for another year. I still dreamed about earning a scholarship and going to France. I worked really hard in 12th grade, and halfway through the year, the French government decided to award five scholarships to the best students by the end of that school year to go to France and study at French universities. The news of scholarships motivated me even more to work harder. I would spend extra hours at our school library to study, do well in my homework and even asked my French teachers for additional homework to become well-prepared for the scholarship exam. Kabir, my classmate and still my rival academically, continued to show his brilliance. Kabir's family started to get involved with the Afghan Resistance movement and there were rumors that he may have also been involved in some anti-government activities. The Afghan Secret Service agents arrested Kabir twice during that final year of high school but released him as the communist regime could not link him to any specific anti-government movements.

Unfortunately, that year, we lost three classmates; they were arrested by the communist regime's Secret Service Agents and no one ever heard back from them again. Their names were Shams, Wais, and Fraidoon. Wais, our class clown and a very smart student made all of us laugh all the time. Fraidoon, a good friend of mine, always talked to me during recess and some days we would sit together and talk about how to study to get a scholarship and leave Afghanistan. Shams, always nicely dressed, tried to be kind to everyone in our class. None of them were affiliated with any anti-government organizations. Our school's Communist Association had a base of hardcore supporters who were mainly related to some powerful communist leaders. Others were either forced to join or joined simply because they were afraid.

We later learned the leaders of sazman-e-jawanan were encouraging their members to spy on anyone who said anything against the government or the Communist Party. During that time, just a minor comment or small criticism of the government could put you in prison or even worse get you killed. It was hard for some people to believe that innocent Afghan people were arrested based on simple anti-communist comments they may have made that got them tortured and killed. We soon learned that our beloved classmates, Shams, Wais and Fraidoon, had been arrested by the Afghan Secret Service agents based on a report from our school's Communist Association stating that they were involved in anti-government activities. They were killed by the communist regime's Secret Service Agents. We all knew for a fact that all three young teenagers were completely innocent and did not belong to any political organizations.

During the first few months, when I started 12th grade, our high school's Afghan principal would walk around the school with a handgun. A completely ignorant communist mad man nicknamed "Amjad," as he looked like a famous scary Indian movie actor. He stalked around school with that handgun. One of the incidents that almost got me and all of my classmates killed happened during Amjad's reign of terror. Since we did not have any known communist sympathizers in our class, one day, one of our classmates mentioned that during the invasions of Czechoslovakia by the Soviet Union, a group of university students started to wear black neckties in protest.

We were still young, naive and idealistic students not knowing that small acts of protest can lead to major tragedies for us and our families. At that time, we were unaware of the fact that three of our beloved classmates had already been killed. A couple of troublemakers in the class proposed that the next day we should all wear black neckties. Everyone agreed, but we had one major problem; finding 25 or 30 black neckties. After some discussion, we decided to just wear a tie, any color tie would do. Not telling my Mom and Baaba the exact reason, I told them that we needed to wear ties for some event at the school. Since my Baaba had to wear suits and ties every day to work, he had a large collection of ties. With his permission the next day, I took a large number of his ties in my backpack to school. Once in school, we counted the number of ties everyone could bring and found out that we did not have enough ties for everyone.

The solution: simply cut a few ties in half and voila, everyone in our class would be wearing a necktie that day. It did not matter if everyone wore a collared shirt, a t-shirt or something else; we all needed to somehow have a tie around our necks. We started our first period with a French teacher, and he found it amusing, not knowing why we were wearing neckties. By the end of the fourth period, the news of our entire class wearing neckties spread all over the high school.

We were in the middle of the fourth period when our crazy Afghan principal, Amjad, with his handgun at his side, along with two other senior Communist Party sympathizers who worked at the school, busted into our classroom. He first ordered our teacher to leave the class. He then took the teacher's seat and took the handgun he was carrying with him out and left it on the desk. One of his comrades who had come with him stood by the door and another one stood in the back of the class. He then started a bizarre and incoherent revolutionary lecture for almost an hour. After his speech, he told us that he had heard from some trusted sources that we were all wearing ties in protest against the revolutionary government. By now, we all were very scared; some had already tried to remove their neckties. But I decided to keep mine on realizing that by now it would not make any difference. He then started asking us why we were wearing the neckties. No one answered. He got really mad. The principal asked one of our classmates, an Indian Afghan Rajadar Kumar, sitting in the front row, the reason for wearing a necktie. Rajandar kept quiet and didn't answer the principal. The principal asked him to stand up and started yelling at him. Scared and worried, he started crying and said he did not know why he was wearing the necktie and thought it would be just a fun thing to do.

Now looking back, I can laugh, but at that time, this terrifying ordeal scared my entire class. The crazy principal responded to Rajandar that he would show him and the rest of us what fun is all about. He then asked another classmate, Hamid, sitting in the front row to stand up. Under the principal's questioning, yelling and screaming at him, Hamid suddenly became very pale, fainted and fell on the floor. I had never seen someone faint in front of me before. The principal, instead of asking someone to help Hamid, loudly and proudly yelled:

"What you just witnessed is the power of our revolution."

Another classmate asked the principal if he could help Hamid, and he replied, "No, let him die." Within a minute or two, we saw Hamid, who still looked quite pale, climb back into his chair.

The principal told us that he would severely punish all of us for our anti-revolutionary act and also that he intended to find out who the real perpetrators behind this "criminal act of protest" were first. He told us that he would start interrogating each student separately to find out the truth and would take appropriate action. He decided to move students from the classroom adjacent to ours to another part of the school and make the adjacent classroom an interrogation room. By now, we were three hours into this scary and terrifying saga. Principal Amjad took his handgun from the teacher's desk and moved to the next classroom to get ready for interrogating us. His two comrades were to stay in our classroom to watch us. We were all terrorized and didn't know what would happen to us. One by one, he asked us to go to the next room for interrogation.

One of the troublemakers in our classroom, Hamidullah, quietly spread a message to all of us that we should all give this maniac and dangerous principal the same answer when interrogated and said that we should tell him that we all wore neckties to celebrate Hamidullah's recent engagement to a young lady. The two other communists who were guarding us were watching all of us with eagle eyes. One of our fellow classmates asked for permission from them to go the bathroom, they clearly and loudly told him no.

By now, a number of students had removed their neckties and since a good number of them were from my father, they had quietly passed them to me and I hid them in the bottom of my backpack. Eventually it became my turn to go and answer questions from the principal. I entered the room and saw him sitting behind the teacher's desk and again he had placed his handgun on the desk in front of him. I felt really scared and nervous. He first asked for my backpack, and I did not know that he also planned to search our backpacks. When he asked for my backpack, knowing that I had a large number of neckties hidden in the bottom of my backpack, I almost passed out, thinking that he would for sure assume that I was one of the instigators. I gave him my backpack and he unzipped one of the larger sections of it, quickly looked inside, and gave it back to me. I felt immensely relieved that he did not find my father's neckties. I believe one of the reasons he could not see the ties at the bottom of my bag because he was crossed-eyed. By now, he had kept us in the school for several hours and all the other students at school had gone home. Since we did not go home on time, some of our parents came and they were waiting behind the school gates looking for us. During the beginning of my interrogation, the communist principal asked me why we wore the neckties; I answered that we all wanted to celebrate Hamidullah, our friend's recent engagement to a young lady. He said:

"You are lying," and continued. "If you tell the truth, you will get life in prison and if you lie, you will be executed."

I didn't know if he used scare tactics to force us to tell him the real reason for all of us wearing neckties or if he might really be serious. When I heard his two harsh punishment options for us, I told myself, I am not sure if life in prison would be better than dying quickly. He kept asking me the same question again and again, and I would give him the same answer. He finally got mad and asked me to get out. I left that interrogation room and went to my regular classroom. After all of us went through the interrogation sessions, the principal came back to our classroom and said that he knew who the real instigators were and would make a decision in the morning. He warned us that he had the power to kill us all and no one would ask him a single question. He finally released us. Exhausted, scared and worried, I walked out to see my Baaba outside of the high school waiting for me. By now, he knew what I had done and he was very upset with me -- and rightfully so. I kept quiet and apologized to him and told him that I would never do anything like that again.

As you can see, we were all living in a constant state of terror. The school year came to an end, and I graduated 12th grade as the valedictorian of our high school in 1980. But, for me, the last exam represented the most important exam of my life, the scholarship exam, scheduled for a few weeks following our official high school graduation. After obtaining my baccalaureate degree, equivalent to a French baccalaureate, I went home and told my Mom that I still need to work hard because I am not done yet. I told her about the five scholarships and that I needed to continue to study. I asked her not to tell anyone else about my next test. During my senior year in high school, in parallel, I also prepared for the entrance exam for the Kabul University. Since there were more high school graduates in Afghanistan than available space at the universities, only top high school graduates passing the university entrance exam had the opportunity to pursue higher education. For me, being admitted at the Kabul University was not even a backup plan.

I wanted to leave Afghanistan because of the political situation, and I had no future there. But regardless, I wanted to take the entrance exam for Kabul University and get a good grade. Since the entrance exam for Kabul University had a different style and requirements from the types of exams we took at my French high school, Mom and Baaba enrolled me in a private tutoring program solely focused on how to succeed and obtain top grades in the Kabul University entrance examination. An ex-university professor named Engineer Osman provided students outstanding training to succeed and obtain top grade in the entrance exam. He had a rare form of dwarfism and people called him "Engineer Osman Landai." Landai means short in Pashtu. I had great respect and admiration for him. As one can imagine, my last year of high school had become very hectic and stressful. After regular school, I would spend my time either going to the private tutoring classes to study for the Kabul University entrance exam or study and do homework for my French high school scholarship exam. Engineer Osman, an extremely bright professor, really knew how to teach and had a unique style of teaching that helped all of his students. He started teaching us mathematics and physics in a very different style, making sure that everyone understood the basic concepts and fundamentals. With a great character and integrity he managed to maintain discipline in large mixed gender classes. All of his students respected him and almost all of his students excelled with top scores at the Kabul University entrance exam. In his youth, Engineer Osman had been involved in politics and had spent many years in prison for opposing the past regimes and their policies.

As I prepared for both exams, I knew what I really wanted to succeed in first, and therefore, I dedicated more time preparing for the French Scholarship exam. I knew Engineer Osman prepared me well for the Kabul University entrance exam too and I could do well, but once again, staying in Kabul did not provide me with a viable option. As military service is mandatory for all young Afghan men, I would have most likely been drafted to fight for the communist regime, as they needed more soldiers to fight the Freedom Fighters. Or I would have been arrested, tortured, or killed like many other young men who did not collaborate with the communist regime. Frequent examples of that were happening in Kabul.

The French Embassy in Kabul scheduled the scholarship exam a week before the Kabul University entrance exam. I was ready for both and could not wait anymore.

I remember the day of the scholarship exam. My Mom, who knew about my plans, woke up early and fixed me a good breakfast. After I did my morning prayer and asked God to help me, I packed my school bag, said good-bye to Mom, and rode my bike to school. When I arrived at school, I noticed everyone looking at me and I felt like a target. There were hundreds of students waiting outside in the school courtyard. After about 10 or 15 minutes, a French teacher divided us into smaller groups and assigned each group to a classroom. I went to my assigned classroom and there were already two French teachers and one person from the French Embassy in that room. I took a seat in the front row of the class. After all the students assigned to my group were seated, one of the French teachers gave us instructions about the test, its duration, and talked about the exam rules in detail. The test had two major parts and we would spend the entire day taking it. In the morning, they focused more on scientific subjects such as Mathematics, Physics, Chemistry, etc., with the afternoon dedicated to Philosophy, French, History, etc.

The tests were really hard, and half of the students did not show up for the afternoon session. I did the best I could but still remained very nervous and anxious after I finished. At the end of the day, we were told that the French teachers would grade all papers and a committee of French educators would examine the overall results. After a complete evaluation, the French Embassy in Kabul would award five students with the highest grades the five available scholarships. A letter from the French Embassy would be sent to the Afghan Ministry of Education with the names of the five students, asking the Ministry to start the administrative process for those students to acquire passports to go to France. All expenses for the selected students, including airfare, would be paid by the French government. The next step would take four to five weeks and that seemed like an eternity for me.

The following week, I went and took the Kabul University entrance exam, a much easier and less stressful experience and I knew I did well. For me, the French Embassy located about 20 minutes from our house by bike became an important place. After a couple of weeks, I could not wait to find out if I would be awarded one of the five scholarships. I went to the French Embassy and asked to talk to someone about the scholarships. One of the embassy employees told me that they did not have the results yet and even if they did, they would not be able to share any information with me. They advised that the Afghan Ministry of Education would be the place to find out more about the names of the top students who would be awarded the scholarships. I went home disappointed, but I am someone who does not give up easily. The following week, I went again to the French Embassy, and this time I talked to an Afghan lady working as a secretary there. She told me that the results should be back within a week. I started to get more nervous and excited at the same time. Waiting for another week looked almost unbearable. In the meantime, the results of the Kabul University entrance exam were posted. As expected, I had done well. But that did not really impact me that much as I waited for the real exam results that could change my life.

A week passed by and I couldn't wait to go back to the French Embassy to see if I could learn about the scholarship test results. This time I went straight to that lady secretary with whom I had spoken the week before. She said the results were in, but she could not share any information with me. I begged her to at least see if the French committee considered me as one of the top five students. She first hesitated and then asked for my name and told me to wait. She went into another office and within a few minutes came out. I looked at her face for any signs. She came close to me and quietly said:

"Yes, your name is on the list; and now please leave before I get in trouble."

I almost started screaming from happiness. I collected myself and ran outside, picked up my bike, and rode home as fast as I could. I dropped my bike and ran to my Mom and told her about the news. She hugged me and told me that she was proud of me. Happy and excited we shared the good news with the rest of the family. I had finally succeeded. The rocket attack, my injuries, major surgeries, hospital stays, my low moments and past depressions did not matter anymore. I finally realized my dream of going to France to get a great education and escape the horrible situation in Afghanistan. I started dreaming about France, the land of *"liberté, égalité, fraternité,"* liberty, equality, and fraternity, where I would no longer be afraid of getting arrested for expressing my opinion, tortured, imprisoned or killed.

Now that I knew that I had been awarded a scholarship to France to study at a French university, I needed to get my passport and permission from the Afghan Ministry of Education and leave. I knew what office at the Afghan Ministry of Education would be responsible for receiving the letter from the French Embassy with our names in order to start the administrative process for us to receive passports and other travel documents to leave the country. I started going to the Ministry of Education every day to see if they had received the letter from the French Embassy. For almost two weeks, I would go twice a day and check; still, no news. Finally, after two weeks, they told me that they had received the letter and, in fact, I had been awarded the French government scholarship, but the Ministry had to do their own due diligence before approving and allowing all five of us students to go. I thought the next step would be just a formality and we should get all the required approvals within a couple of weeks. Little did I know how wrong that idea could be.

Since everything had become politicized during that time, the Afghan communist regime did not appreciate young people who refused to join the youth communist organizations in schools. Young students with any ties to anti-government movements were arrested, tortured, and killed. The first step for allowing the top five students who were awarded the French scholarships to go to France became the most problematic issue for me. They asked the main communist student organization at our school for their approval. Since I had refused to join the school's Communist Association after repeated requests by some of their members, I had come to be regarded as an "unpatriotic" member of the society.

A week later, during one of my daily visits to the Ministry of Education, they told me that the ministry decided that my name should be dropped from the list of students who were awarded the scholarships. One of the staff told me the Ministry of Education had sent a letter to the French Embassy informing them that this student (me) did not meet the Afghan government standards and criteria for being awarded a scholarship.

I felt totally devastated.

I believed strongly that they had robbed me of my life, and my legs did not have the energy to walk down the stairs, pick up my bike and ride home. Somehow, I managed to get home and went to give the bad news to my Mom. I collapsed in her arms and started crying uncontrollably. She asked me about what happened and I told her the entire story.

They were getting ready to have lunch and she told me to eat something and swore that she would fight with every fiber of her being to make sure they didn't rob me of my scholarship. My Baaba and the rest of the family were also shocked by the news, and they all said that they would do everything in their power to salvage my scholarship.

After lunch, Mom, Baaba and I took a taxi to the Ministry of Education. We went straight to the office of one of the vice presidents of the Ministry of Education, a hard-core communist in charge of issues related to scholarships. His name was Wafamal. We were not sure of his level of education, but for sure he knew how to wear a nice suit and put on a colorful necktie. His secretary told us that Mr. Wafamal was busy with someone in his office. My Mom did not hesitate for a second and opened his office door while the secretary protested. We all entered. He appeared to be enjoying and having a good time with a woman, laughing, talking, and drinking tea. He looked a bit shocked and he asked why we were in his office. Mom told him that we were there because of a major injustice he had been caused by denying a smart high school student, the valedictorian of his school selected by the French teachers as one of the top five students to receive a scholarship to go in pursuit of his college education to France. Mom continued to say that I had met all required standards by the French and it fell fully within my rights to receive my awarded scholarship. Wafamal, with his heavy thick moustache, started laughing and told Mom:

"Your son has not met our standard of patriotism."

Mom, in a loud voice, responded:

"Your standards of so called 'patriotism' allow people like you to sit in that chair under the protection of the Russian soldiers."

Baaba and I were getting a bit scared that we might be arrested. Baaba pulled Mom aside and told her that we should leave. The woman in Wafamal's office told Mom to behave like a "dignified" person in front of a high ranking official.

Mom told her to be quiet as it was not her business and she would not allow an entertainer like her to lecture her about dignity.

Baaba finally succeeded in pulling Mom out of that office. When we left, Baaba told Mom that even if we had a tiny chance of saving the scholarship, she had ruined it by talking to that communist vice president in such a harsh manner. Mom, still angry and even more determined, told Baaba that she would not let them get away with this type of injustice. We took another taxi and went home. During the ride home, they were brainstorming on what the next step should be, who else we could contact, and any other member of the regime that someone we knew could talk to who might help us. I lost hope again became upset and didn't know what to do. This setback as one of the lowest points of my life made me feel powerless and dismayed.

The next day I went to the French Embassy and asked to talk to someone there to see if they could help. The cultural attaché of the embassy, a nice French gentleman called me into his office and saw how distraught and disappointed I had become. He first told me that, unfortunately, the French Embassy could not force the Afghan Education Ministry to do anything they were not willing to do. He asked me to keep a positive attitude and work through the Ministry of Education to find a solution. He did not say it directly, but he hinted that somehow if I could manage to get out of Afghanistan, they would honor my scholarship and send me to France from another country. During that time a large number of Afghans were escaping the country through borders with Pakistan and once in Pakistan, they were applying for asylum to other countries through their embassies.

I left the French Embassy and rode my bike to my high school. I wanted to go and talk to the new high school principal and see if he could help me. He was also a communist, but from a different faction of the party than the Vice President Wafamal (I did not know that at the time). Our new high school principal named Hamdard had graduated from our high school and spent some time in France receiving training. Although a communist principal, Hamdard was different from other communist leaders. He seemed like a fair and honest man and did not like or approve some of the policies of his own government, including mass arrests, torture, imprisonment and killing of the ordinary Afghans who were not supportive of their regime.

I went to his office and his secretary told me that I needed to wait as someone else had a meeting with him. After waiting for a few minutes, the other person left his office and he asked me to come in. I went into his office and explained what had happened. He already knew that I graduated as the valedictorian of my high school that year and knew me as a good student. Surprised and shocked that the Ministry of Education had not approved my awarded French scholarship, he asked me if they offered me any explanation. I told him that since I did not join the school Communist Association, they considered me as "unpatriotic." I also told him about our visit to Vice President Wafamal, and suddenly he got even more upset. As I mentioned, Wafamal belonged to different faction of the party and he was not on good terms with him. He picked up the phone and called the office of the Minister of Education. He knew the minister personally through their party committees. He told the minister the entire story and reminded him that the reason he started his struggle and became a member of the party was to fight injustice and corruption. The high school principal insinuated that Vice President Wafamal may have become somehow involved in corruption and injustice and may have had the intention of giving my scholarship to someone else close to him.

Obviously, the minister did not know anything about this, and he asked Principal Hamdard to come and see him immediately. Principal Hamdard hung up the phone and told me to go with him and see the minister. I could not believe the new turn of events and became even a bit shocked, scared and worried about what the minister would say. After about 10 minutes, we arrived in the waiting room of the Minister of Education. By the time we arrived there, the minister had already talked to Vice President Wafamal, who had arrived in his office.

When Principal Hamdard and I entered the minister's office, he had a folder in front of him. He asked us to sit down. The minister opened that folder and it appeared that he had already gone through the files and asked Principal Hamdard if he really knew what kind of a person I was? Principal Hamdard, in a very confident voice told him that he is a hardworking, intelligent, bright student and graduated as valedictorian. He continued that no one is more qualified than him to receive this scholarship. Hearing such kind words was very humbling to me. The minister then asked him:

"Is he a patriot?"

"Yes, of course, he is."

Principal Hamdard continued to repeat what he told the minister over the phone:

"We sacrificed our lives to fight injustice and corruption and he reminded him that during the Monarchy, only the king and his family were awarded these types of privileges and now we need to make sure that people who truly deserve them should be rewarded."

Silence took over the room and no one talked for another minute or two. The minister asked me to leave his office and wait outside. I quickly left the office and waited in the waiting room. Not sure exactly what they were talking about and would happen next, I decided to stay calm and wait and see. After about five minutes, Principal Hamdard came out and asked me to come into the office of the minister.

The minister asked me about the mandatory military service that all young men have to do. I told him that I was badly injured during the "Revolution" (their military coup) and I would most likely be exempted from military service. At the bottom of a piece of paper, he ordered that my scholarship should only be approved if I got an exemption from military service. We all got out of the minister's office and I walked outside with Principal Hamdard. He handed me the order of the minister and we walked back to the high school.

I now had a glimmer of hope. I went home and told Mom and Baaba about what had happened. They were both optimistic that now we had an opening and they would take care of this military service exemption. Military service record keeping in Afghanistan still relied on large volumes of paper and an office dedicated to record keeping kept track of all young men in Kabul who were exempt from mandatory military service. Then one of my Baaba's cousins named Haji Najeeb, who lived in the north in the city of Tashkurgan, came to visit us that day. Baaba explained the saga of my scholarship to him. He asked Baaba and me to go with him to the military record keeping office and see if we could do something. We took a taxi and arrived at an old building with a large hangar-style office full of papers everywhere. We arrived during lunch time and only the director of the Record Keeping Office was there. Out of nowhere, Haji Najeeb started to hug the director and told him that so and so was our ancestor, and we were distant cousins. Then Baaba also started hugging the director. At first, I thought he had some family relationship with us and later on learned that Haji Najeeb tried to trick him to make that director be more welcoming and friendly with us.

Anyway, I am not sure if the director of the Military Record Keeping Office believed my Baaba or Haji Najeeb, but he said we could go through all the records and see if my name was in one of the documents that listed people who were exempt from the military service. I had never applied for any military exemptions before since I was too young to be drafted. I was more than certain that my name would not be found in any documents. The office, full of papers from floor to ceiling, looked extremely disorganized.

We started to look at the lists. I hoped that by going through the thousands of names, we might find a name similar to mine and then the director might give us a military exemption paper. While we were looking, I noticed Haji Najeeb in a corner of the room working on a large pile of documents. Surely he was up to something. Within 10 or 15 minutes, he brought a small stack of papers and put it in front of the director on his desk. We all three continued to look through the names, and after a few minutes the director asked me:

"What is your name again?"

I repeated my name, and he said, "Here it is!" My name somehow magically had appeared on one of the sheets of paper that Haji Najeeb worked on mysteriously in the corner and had brought to the director. All the names in the record document were handwritten in different types of pens and different styles of handwriting. The director took an official military exemption form, wrote my name on it, and asked about the reason for my exemption. I quickly showed him my scars from my past injuries and he wrote "medical reason" on the exemption form. He signed and stamped the form and we were done!

Without any delay, we brought that exemption form to the Ministry of Education. A director in the scholarship bureau quickly typed an official request to the Ministry of Foreign Affairs requesting a passport for me to travel to France. During that time, all students going abroad on scholarships would receive a "Service Passport." The Ministry of Foreign Affairs Service Passports issued Service Passports mostly to Afghan diplomats and officials.

The trip from the Ministry of Education to the Ministry of Foreign Affairs only took a few minutes. We were getting closer to the end of the day and I told Baaba that I would take the passport request letter and run quickly to make sure they issued my passport before they left for the day. I ran like a maniac and arrived at the passport office of the Ministry of Foreign Affairs. I showed my papers and already had two picture IDs ready with me. They took everything and since they were getting ready to leave the office for the day, they told me to come back in the morning on Sunday (a working day in Afghanistan).

A bit disappointed, I walked out of the ministry and saw that Baaba had just arrived. I told him what happened and he asked me to wait outside while he went inside the ministry. I waited for almost 40 minutes and finally saw Baaba coming out. He told me that we needed to come back as they could not issue the passport that day. We went home and still a bit nervous, not sure what else could go wrong with issuing the passport, I finally had some glimmer of hope. We told Mom how we got the military exemption and the final approval from the Ministry of Education and now we were waiting for my passport. I saw a smirk on Baaba's face and he started saying a quote:

"Even if you are Alexander the Great, do not go to a battle without a wise man."

Then he put his hand in his pocket and showed me my passport.

I suddenly became the happiest person on the face of the earth that evening; nothing could dampen my excitement.

Since Baaba had worked in the Ministry of Foreign Affairs many years ago, he still had some friends there. When he had gone inside, he had found one of his old friends who decided to issue my passport without delay.

The next morning I went to the French Embassy and told them that I finally had my passport and felt ready to go. The four other students who were awarded the same scholarships were already in France. The French Embassy's Cultural Attaché, who had seen me several weeks ago, appeared really happy to see me smiling, congratulated me and he told his staff to make my travel arrangements as soon as possible. The French Embassy scheduled my flight from Kabul to Paris for the following week. I simply could not wait!

A couple of days before my flight, I went to see Principal Hamdard in his home to say thank you and goodbye. He lived in a modest home in a suburb of Kabul. He greeted me warmly and told me that he just did his job and it made him happy to correct and injustice. He wished me good luck with my new life in France and asked me to continue working hard as Afghanistan needed people like me. Before saying good bye, he asked me to come back and see him during the summer breaks. I also went to see Engineer Osman, the private tutor who prepared students for the Kabul University entrance exam. He did not know about my French Scholarship award, but told me that it did not surprise him as he viewed me as a bright student and that comment coming from him made me very happy.

The night before my flight to Paris, I had mixed feeling: of happiness for finally realizing my dream of earning a full-paid scholarship to France, escaping war and an uncertain future, and also a feeling of sadness to leave my loved ones behind under an extremely oppressive regime in a country where thousands of innocent people were in prison for political reasons or had been killed. But I felt powerless to change anything for them that could help them. I told myself that by getting a good education, I could become more helpful to my family and my people.

The next morning, on a nice sunny spring day in Kabul, I woke up and got ready for my journey to travel to Europe. My flight was scheduled to depart Kabul around 11:00 am local time, and Mom had already packed my luggage. I finally realized that it happened and I am going to France. I did not know if I would ever return to Afghanistan. All members of my family went to the airport with me that morning, and when it came time to say goodbye, almost everyone started to cry -- not sure if they would ever see me again, not sure of what would happen to them, not sure of their future, but they were happy that I at least managed to escape the uncertain future and would be going to a safe country.

114

I said my goodbyes and kissed everyone, walked to the passport checkpoint, still nervous that they might find something wrong and stop me from going. After all, nothing had been going smoothly for me, so I still felt unsettled. The agent looked at my passport and saw that I had a Service Passport; he did not say anything else and wished me a nice flight. I got out of the terminal and walked towards the airplane, waving to my loved ones who now were in the balcony of the terminal watching me board the airplane. I found my seat and waited for the plane to take off.

That was the last time I saw the beautiful mountains of Afghanistan, about 36 years ago.

7 BEAUTIFUL FRANCE – CAEN, BORDEAUX, MONTPELLIER, PARIS

After a few hours into our flight to Paris the captain announced that we had entered the European air space. That's when I finally realized that no way would I now be stopped from pursuing my dreams.

After about 7 or 8 hours in the air, another announcement by the captain informed passengers that we were approaching Paris. It had turned night time there and I could see the shiny stars in the perfect blue sky through the window of the airplane. Once we got closer to Paris, I realized why Paris is called the city of lights. From the sky I could see lights everywhere, in every corner of Paris. The lower the plane flew the more structures and buildings I could see.

I saw the lighted beautiful Eiffel Tower that I had first seen on that post card given to me as a reward by my first French teacher. I also saw the Arc de Triumph for the first time. I thought this is like being in a dream as I rubbed my eyes to make sure that I really had arrived in Paris. The scene of seeing Paris from the sky felt overwhelming. I now knew for sure that I had made it and my dream of going to France had become a reality. We finally landed at the Orly International Airport of Paris. I went through immigration, picked up my luggage, and walked out of the terminal.

My four other friends and classmates who were also awarded the same scholarships were waiting for me at the airport. I felt happy and excited to see them. We were all assigned to spend our first three months in the north of France in a city called Caen, a small city about an hour and half north of Paris in Normandy. Since I arrived late that night, I decided to spend my first night in Paris. One of my friends' brothers, who had come several years earlier, lived in Paris, and I spent my first night in France at his apartment in downtown Paris with my friend and his brother. My three other friends decided to go back to Caen that night.

I woke up early in the morning and wanted to go out and see Paris for the first time. My friend and I went to a small boulangerie or bakery on the corner of the street to buy some fresh French baguettes, croissants, and some pastries. For the first time, I tasted a freshly warm croissant and that savoring taste felt insanely addictive. I did not have much time to visit Paris that day as I needed to be in Caen to take care of my scholarship paperwork. After breakfast, I packed my stuff and headed to the train station with my friend to catch the train to Caen.

We first took the Metro, a first nice experience looking at different faces of people going to start their journey in this beautiful city. We arrived at the train station and bought one-way train tickets to Caen. I had never been on a train before and with excitement looked forward to my train trip to Caen. We left Paris for Caen in the morning, another nice trip going through beautiful small towns and villages. I watched cows and other farm animals roaming on green pastures and saw picturesque hilltops showing the beauty of my new country. Normandy is well-known for its dairy products and many different varieties of cheeses.

We arrived in Caen in late morning and went straight to the office in charge of foreign students with a French scholarship. The ladies in the office were very welcoming. After filling out some forms, they assigned me a room in a dorm and also gave me some money for food and other miscellaneous expenses. I took my belongings and went to the dorm. The dorm rooms were all single-occupancy rooms, very comfortable with a nice bed, a desk and a sink in the corner of the room. All my friends were in the same dorm and that made me a bit more comforted as I did not feel lonely. After arriving in my room and settling down I quickly started to write a letter home, telling them that I had arrived safely, everything went well during my trip and I missed them already. I went to the local post office and sent the letter home.

Caen is a small, quiet, charming city in Normandy. The plan for the five of us: spend our first three months there to learn more about the French culture, and history and get acclimated. We were also taken on several excursions to visit many historical sites in Normandy and the northern region of France. One of the excursions included a trip to the beautiful island monastery of Mont St. Michel from the 11th century. It's an amazing structure built of stones up high, about 1 kilometer offshore at the mouth of Couesnon River. The island has held strategic fortifications since ancient times and since the 8th century AD has been the seat of the monastery from which it draws its name. It attracts millions of tourists each year.

During the first few days in Caen, because of the significant time difference between Kabul and Caen, I had difficulty sleeping at night. At night all five of us gathered in one of our dorm rooms and played cards, listened to music, and sometimes just went for walks outside in the middle of the night and then slept most of the day. Walking outside after curfew had not been possible in Kabul, and those midnight walks gave us a sense of freedom that we had taken for granted before. Caen had a very small Afghan community, formed mainly by other Afghan students from our high school who had arrived several years before us. We quickly became friends with a young Afghan student named Nasser. He studied at the University of Caen and had been in Caen for several years before we arrived. He had a French girlfriend named Patricia. They were very friendly, nice and fun to be around. They lived in a small studio apartment outside of the campus and we spent most of our free time with them.

Nasser had an Iranian-made rice cooker and we spent countless nights at his place eating rice with fish or chicken, playing cards and having fun. Nasser's older brother also lived with them. He had been granted asylum to stay in France by the French government. He also was a very nice and kind person and enjoyed spending time with the five of us new Afghan students in town.

We were experiencing the end of the spring season and the beginning of the summer season in Caen. The weather remained beautiful. Some days we would have fun at the beach and other days we would play soccer with Nasser and his Iranian friends. By that time one my uncles, Uncle Hamed lived in Switzerland. He had arrived there as a refugee a couple of years ahead of us. I sent him a letter and he really felt happy that I had left our country and lived in France. We talked on the phone when we could, and he finally found some free time to come and visit me once. Uncle Hamed was in his mid to late 20s at that time, a kind and loving Uncle. He loved the beach and when he arrived, he quickly bonded with all of my friends and we all went to the beach in Normandy. His nice visit didn't last long. But now I knew that I had a loved one not too far I could count on if I needed anything. Before leaving for Switzerland, he bought me some nice shirts and shoes despite my protests.

As a refugee, he worked hard and I did not want him to waste his money on me. Once I lost my wallet with all of my money and documents -- at the beginning of the month and that meant I had no money to pay my dorm rent or buy food. I called Uncle Hamed and when he learned what had happened to me, he quickly sent me money and that helped me greatly during that time of desperation. He always tried to help me, making sure I did well in school and did not get too homesick. I also tried to talk to Uncle Abdul and his wife in America over the phone whenever I could and with Uncle Hamed, as they were my family outside of Afghanistan that I could talk to on a regular basis. We really enjoyed our first few months in Caen; it was relaxing, fun and we were all together and did not feel too lonely despite being far from our loved ones. By the end of that summer of 1981, things were about to change as we were assigned to different parts of France to start our real education.

I got assigned to Bordeaux, a large city in southwestern France. Bordeaux is known for its wine. It is also a large port city with a population of more than one million people. The education plan for foreign students like us involved redoing our last year of high school, called Terminal, in a French high school to ensure that we were all ready to start our University education on solid academic grounds.

Since we came from a French high school in Afghanistan and were regarded as top students, we were all assigned to great high schools. In the French educational system at that time, students with higher academic achievements were grouped together. Therefore, all five of us were assigned to excellent high schools and also were assigned to classes with brilliant students. Unfortunately for us, that last year of high school in Afghanistan had been very tumultuous because of the political situation in the country and that did not help us learn to the same level of academic standards of French high school students.

I left Caen on an early morning in August, saying goodbyes to all of my friends and took the train to Bordeaux. I arrived in Bordeaux in late afternoon and went to the office of foreign students. Everything in Bordeaux seemed different. Even the way people spoke French was different. They had a different accent not familiar to me.

After filling out some paper work, I received my dorm room assignment. My high school, "Lycée Camille Jullian," stood on the opposite side of the town, a long way from my dorm. School would start in a few weeks, so I had some time to figure things out. I took two buses to reach my new dorm. I arrived at the dorm exhausted.

But again the dorm rooms were single occupancy, very nice and comfortable. I collapsed on the bed in my room and took a nap. After my quick nap, I decided to go out and explore the campus and also to find a place to eat. As I left my room, I noticed the sound of music coming from the end of the long hallway. It sounded like Afghan music. I told myself that I must be dreaming. I did not know any Afghans in Bordeaux and how improbable it would have been that someone in my dorm floor would listen to Afghan music. I locked my dorm room and decided to check out where that music came from. The closer I got to the end of that hallway, the more amazed I became, as that Afghan music featured a famous Afghan singer, Ahmad Zaher, who had been killed by the Afghan communist regime. When I got in front of that dorm room where the music came, my heart beat really hard, not knowing who would be inside that room.

I collected myself and knocked on the door. The door opened, and right in front of me stood an old high school friend of mine, Hamid. Hamid and I were classmates before I got injured and he came to France on a scholarship a year earlier. We were both shocked and hugged each other and would not let each other go. He had begun preparing dinner for himself on a portable gas stove and invited me to have dinner with him. I stayed in his room, had dinner with him and talked almost all night about everything -- school, life in Bordeaux, the small Afghan community there, etc. He also told me that he planned to move to Montpellier, a small college town in the south of France.

That news felt a bit disappointing, that he planned to leave Bordeaux, but I felt happy for him as I had heard great reviews from other students about Montpellier and its universities. Hamid moved to Montpellier the following week, not knowing that I would be joining him a year later. He was a very sharp and hardworking student. Short in stature, he had a black moustache which moved in a funny way with his unique laughter and had dark black hair. Hamid was also one of the best cooks among all of us and he had a very unique way of entertaining us all with his jokes, laughter, funny stories, and bringing joy to us all.

Hamid studied Electrical Engineering, earning an undergraduate degree and then completed his master's degree in Computer Science at one of the Universities in Paris. By the time he completed his master's degree, his family had immigrated to the United States because of the war in Afghanistan. Hamid had decided to join his family in America and after obtaining his green card, he moved to New Jersey where his family had settled. In a tragic turn of events, two years after arriving to America, Hamid had been diagnosed with leukemia and passed away at a very young age. I was devastated when I learned about the sad news and my heart still misses him till this day, remembering his vivacious personality and friendship. I remember his laughter, his cute sense of humor, his hard work and dedication to his studies and his love for his family. I already knew that Hamid had lost his father when he was just a teenager, and I could not imagine in what state his Mom would have been after losing her son. He died too young and it felt heartbreaking.

I felt overwhelmed and alone in this large city of Bordeaux, not knowing anyone, living far from my school. A day after my arrival there, I decided to find my high school. I had to take two buses, and it took me more than an hour and 15 minutes from my dorm to get there. The high school sat in an old historic building and at first it looked like a haunted house to me. I went to the administration building to get some details about my class assignment and school calendar. By now, I felt fluent in French. A lady in the administration office gave me the information I needed. I had been assigned to a class of Terminal "C." Students in Terminal "C" were all extremely bright and highly intelligent students. I felt ready for the next chapter of my life. Without knowing ahead of time, however, my resilience and strength were about to be tested once again.

Within a few weeks, school started. I had to get up really early as I needed to take two buses, and it took me more than an hour and 15 minutes to get to school now, because of additional traffic on the roads. The first day, I went to my class and did not know anyone and quietly took a seat. It appeared that everyone else knew each other and they were talking and laughing. Once in a while, someone would say "Hi" to me. A girl sat next to me and asked for my name. I told her my name and asked for her name and learned that she also came new in the class. Her family had just moved to Bordeaux from another region of France. I told her that I came from Afghanistan. I don't think she knew much about Afghanistan and she did not ask too many questions.

I soon realized that school would be really hard; I mean, really, really hard for someone like me. The pace of teaching felt much faster than I had experienced and I needed to work extra hard to keep up with that faster pace. The first math exam became a real eye opener for me. Our math teacher was a tall skinny lady with short brown hair, round eyes wearing thick prescription eye glasses and her name was Mademoiselle

Chaumet. She appeared to be in her late 50s and never smiled, always very serious looking and required all students to over perform in her class. After a few weeks of teaching, we had our first four-hour math test. It was a hard test for me and I tried to do the best I could. I wasn't really sure if I did well, but was about to find out. A week later, Mademoiselle Chaumet brought back our graded test papers. She had this habit of sorting graded papers from highest grades on top of the pile to the lowest grades in the bottom. She started distributing graded papers, first giving students with top grades their papers without any comments or compliments and then started to distribute graded papers with lowest marks, lecturing each student who did not do well on what they missed and what they needed to do to improve their grades.

My paper came last.

She called my name and I raised my hand. She approached me and I remember to this day exactly what she said, in a very sarcastic voice as she called my name:

"Now, the genius of the class . . ."

She started talking about all of my mistakes and told me that I really needed to work hard or I would fail in her class. My grade was either 40 or 50, the lowest grade of the class. I noticed that some students were laughing at her sneering remarks. I almost had tears in my eyes and wanted to dig a hole in the ground and hide. Other students with lowest grades didn't care, as they were all smart and brilliant students and knew that they would recover in the next exam. Mademoiselle Chaumet noticed that her comments really affected me. It was the last period of the day. After the class ended and everyone left, Mademoiselle Chaumet came to me and asked to me stay in the classroom.

She went and closed the class door and took a chair and came to sit next to me. She asked me from what region of France I moved from. I told her I was from Afghanistan on a scholarship to go the University in France. She seemed shocked. It was the first time she saw an Afghan in her class during her long teaching career. She then asked me about my family, where I lived, how I got to school and spent almost an hour quizzing me about different topics. She moved her chair facing me then and looked at me in the eyes and said:

"Here is what we will do to help you. From now on, you need to arrive at school an hour early every day in the morning and leave an hour late. I will work with you personally to help you succeed and I want you to do your part. I will give you extra homework and will give you useful books, but you need to work hard."

After hearing my whole story and what I had gone through, she said:

"Academically, your classmates may be ahead of you, but you are way ahead of them in life."

Mademoiselle Chaumet had become my mentor, my private tutor, and treated me like a son as she watched my determination to work hard and learn from her. She was not married and did not have kids, but was an angel that God had sent to me that day.

From that day on, I woke up at 5:00 am in the morning, making sure to be in school early and Mademoiselle Chaumet was always there waiting for me to start work immediately. She worked with me before and after school not only on math, but other school subjects like physics, biology, chemistry and even philosophy. She even would buy books from her own money for me and I will never forget her kindness.

A couple of months later, we had another major four-hour test. Mademoiselle Chaumet started distributing test papers and my paper was again last. I started to freak out and told myself this was going to be very disappointing. Mademoiselle Chaumet called my name and came close to me and handed me my paper. I had the top grade in the class. She wasn't the type of a person to praise students too much for their hard work and high grades. That day she put one of her hands on my shoulder and told me that she was really proud of me. I knew her compliments came scarce, so at that moment, I was the happiest student alive. The scholarship office wanted a monthly progress report from the school. Mademoiselle Chaumet wrote a long report for me that month stating that I was one of her best students she had ever had and with my hard work and dedication, she firmly believed that I could achieve great success in life.

Another major surprise that year in Bordeaux came in the form of a visit from my Baaba. Since he no longer worked in the government, he had managed to obtain a passport to explore the possibility of starting an import/export business, mainly looking into exporting handmade Afghan rugs and importing goods from Europe into Afghanistan. One night, while I studied in my dorm room, someone knocked on my door; I opened the door and there was my Baaba standing right in front of me. A total surprise, I hugged him and felt super excited to see him with tears of happiness rolling down our faces.

I took a couple of days off from school and went to Paris with Baaba where one of his cousins lived. After spending some time in Paris, Baaba went to Switzerland to see Uncle Hamed to discuss his business ideas with him and then headed back to Kabul.

When Baaba arrived in Bordeaux, I had purchased an old small motorcycle to cut down my commute time to school. The motorcycle was not very reliable and would break down often, but on most days, it would take me to and from school faster than taking two buses. When Baaba saw that I had a motorcycle, he said he worried that I might get into a road accident; that I could get hurt badly. He advised me to sell my motorcycle and gave me some money to buy a small used car. His wishes were granted, as two weeks after he left, someone stole my motorcycle. I decided to buy a small cheap car. After looking for a reliable, but inexpensive car, I finally found an old French Citroën "*Deux Chevaux*" or Citroën 2CV car that another student wanted to sell for 500 Francs. I did have the money; the car seemed to be okay, and I decided to buy it.

The Citroën 2CV cars were very popular in France when they were first made in the late 1940s. On some models, the entire top of the car was made of some type of a plastic material that could be removed very easily (cheap man's convertible), and mine was one of those. The engine was small and not too complicated and did not consume too much gasoline. I quickly obtained my driver's license and soon learned that I needed to also have liability insurance for my car. When I went to a few insurance agencies, I discovered that it was impossible for me to afford liability insurance. Now, I was stuck with that car and could not afford insurance but needed to use it. I first made some short trips to learn all the roads that were not too crowded with cars and slowly got more courage and drove that car without liability insurance, not realizing how risky and dangerous that could be. But I was young and had survived many other dangerous situations -- driving a car without insurance was a risk I was willing to take.

Toward the end of the school year, I started to have some new problems with my leg. I went to see an orthopedic surgeon, and after a thorough examination, he determined that one of the titanium screws in my thigh had somehow become infected, and I had to go through another major surgery to remove the titanium plate and all the screws, as my bones had healed; no need for the plate and screws to hold my bones in place. The operation successful left me without anyone to help after such a fairly major surgery. I moved back into my dorm and had a couple of rough weeks until I completely recovered.

The school year ended successfully and I prepared to enter the university. One of my best friends, Akram, who had finished his Terminal "C" in Caen, and I decided to apply to the University of Montpellier. We were both admitted to the University of Montpellier and we both decided to move there. Before leaving Bordeaux, I went to see Mademoiselle Chaumet and told her that I decided to move to Montpellier. She felt sad that I would leave Bordeaux but happy for me because Montpelier was a nice small college town with great universities. She wished me good luck and asked me to keep in touch.

On an early August morning in 1982, I loaded my Citroën 2CV with all my belongings and started to drive towards Montpellier. The drive from Bordeaux to Montpellier is a four and half to five hour drive with a nice normal car, but with my Citroën 2CV it would be a long seven to eight hour journey. Young and fearless, I decided to drive, hoping that my car would make it to my destination. The day felt hot and sunny. Knowing that I did not have liability insurance for my car, I drove with extra care on the highways. After a few hours, I stopped in a small village for a quick 10-minute break and then continued, frequently checking the road map I had to make sure I took the right roads. I stopped for lunch mid-way through my journey and towards the beginning of the evening, I started seeing signs that I should be getting close to Montpellier.

I felt really tired because the driver seat of my car had been broken on one side in the back and I had used a piece of wood to hold the seat fairly straight and stable – not comfortable at all. I continued to drive on the main highway towards Montpelier and on a stretch of the highway after going uphill for a while; I reached the top of the hilly highway road.

Then my car started to go downhill really fast. I put my foot on the brake pedal as the car started to go faster and faster. I pushed my foot harder and harder on the brake pedal. All of a sudden, I heard the sound of something cracking or breaking and quickly realized that my brake pedal felt really soft and no matter how hard I pushed, it would not do anything.

I realized that I had lost my brakes and my car was still going downhill at a very fast speed. I thought that this was it:

I had not died during a rocket attack.

I did not die riding my old motorcycle.

But now I felt destined to die in this uncontrollable old Citroën 2 CV on a French highway. I managed to keep control of the car and once I got closer to the bottom of the hilly highway road, I remembered my parking brakes. Without even thinking for a second, I pulled the handle of my parking brakes as hard as I could. I heard a screeching noise caused by my car's tires and saw my car spinning around a couple of times and then stopping on the shoulder of the road.

I soon got out of the car and started to calm down. I looked around the car to see if there was any damage and could not see anything. I also realized how lucky I had been to have not gotten hit by another car. Luckily the traffic had been very light on that portion of the highway. I did not know what to do, as I had never experienced anything like this in my life before and started to think about a solution. I decided to go under the dashboard of the car and look at the brake pedal to see what was wrong. When I lowered myself to check the brake pedal, I saw a broken metallic pin that held the brake paddle connected to the two solid ends of a system, allowing that peddle to be pushed down and retract.

Even without any mechanical experience, I felt fairly certain I had found the problem. I started to look for a piece of metal similar to that broken pin to see if somehow I could temporarily fix my problem and continue driving to Montpellier. I don't know how, after looking around on the ground for about 30 minutes, I found an old rusted nail and tried to insert it to replace that broken pin. To my surprise, that old rusted nail fit in that hole and when I pushed the brake paddle, it seemed to work. I test drove the car on the shoulder of the highway for a short distance and tried the brakes several times and they worked. Without any more delay, I continued my trip back on the highway, driving at a much slower speed and with great care.

Within about 10 or 15 minutes, I noticed a French police officer on motorcycle flashing his lights behind my car. After what I had gone through, I really didn't need to be stopped by a police officer, especially knowing that I did not have liability insurance. I pulled my car to the side of the highway, scared and worried, and not sure what would happen to me. I pulled down my window and saw that this tall, muscular police officer with an extraordinary large moustache looking at me and asking for my driver's license, vehicle registration, and insurance papers. I quickly gave him my driver's license and car's registration card, but did not tell him that I did not carry liability insurance for my car. I pretended that I frantically searched for my liability insurance documents. After a minute or so, he asked me if I knew why he had stopped me. I said no, I had no idea. He first mentioned a broken tail light and the fact that I drove very slowly on a high-speed highway. I apologized for the broken tail light and told him that I planned to replace it as soon as I arrived in Montpellier. Regarding my driving speed, I told him that I just tried to be extra careful. He took my driver's license and my car's registration card and told me to look for my insurance paper while he verified my documents. Within a couple of minutes, he came back to my car and with a completely different demeanor. He asked me:

"Are you Afghan?"

"Yes," I replied, knowing the place of birth indicated in the French driver's license. He took his helmet off and started to ask me questions about Afghanistan, the Soviet invasion, the Mujahedin, etc. He seemed genuinely interested in knowing more about me and Afghanistan. He told me that it was his first time meeting an Afghan as he had always admired the people of Afghanistan and had heard so many great stories about the bravery of the Afghan people fighting the Soviet Union. He asked me how I got to France and I told him about my scholarship and going to Montpellier starting my university education. By then, he had become much friendlier and I felt more at ease talking to him.

I decided to come clean and tell him that I did not have liability insurance for my vehicle as I could not afford it.

He seemed surprised that I gave him that information that I did not tell him when he had first stopped me. I tried to explain to him that my scholarship money was not enough for me to purchase liability insurance. He calmly explained to me how dangerous it was to drive a car without insurance and advised me to either obtain insurance or sell my car as he did not want me to get into major troubles. He took a small piece of paper and wrote his name on it with his phone number and told me to call him if I ran into any problems. He also wrote the name and phone number of a lady in Montpellier who could possibly help me with the liability insurance for my car. He continued to tell me to drive carefully until I got to my destination and then stop driving until I obtained liability insurance. He gave my papers back to me and wished me good luck and asked me again to be careful. Obviously, he did not issue a citation and I was ecstatic. I slowly continued driving towards Montpellier and arrived there later that evening.

In Montpellier, I spent the first night at my best friend Akram's place who had arrived a couple of weeks earlier, and the following morning I went to the foreign student office to obtain a room in the same dorm as Akram. I next went to the university to officially register and obtain my student card. By the end of the second day, I had completed all administrative tasks and felt ready to start college. My dorm room was in the same building where Akram lived. There was a nice cafeteria outside of the dorm and I was happy and really motivated to start strong and do well in school.

In the fall of 1982, I started my studies at the University of Montpellier. Akram and I decided to study Electrical Engineering. School was again not easy and we had to work very hard to succeed. The university was located across from our dorm and we just walked to classes. I learned to become very organized quickly and created a study routine for myself to make sure I did not fall behind. As I had always been an early morning person -- even on weekends I woke up early and after some exercises would eat breakfast, then go to an empty classroom inside the university and review all my work for the week or try to get ready for any upcoming tests. When my friends would see me going to the university on weekends, they would tease me and often asked me what I was doing inside an empty classroom. But that was my way of concentrating and learning and it worked well for me. After we arrived in Montpellier, a larger group of young Afghan students moved there. It was really fun to have a small Afghan community away from home. For the large part, we got along really well with each other.

I became really close to a couple of Afghan students, Tor and Homayoun. Tor was a great friend, hardworking, who had gone through really hard times. He had spent some time in prison under the communist regime in Kabul, accused of being an antigovernment activist. He was tortured and beaten badly several times during his captivity. But he always stayed positive and worked hard. Tor was a genuine friend with a big heart. Today, he lives in the United States, has two young boys and is happily married.

Homayoun was my philosopher friend. We talked politics, as he studied political science and philosophy. I really enjoyed his conversations about religions, God, politics, and loved his sense of humor. After obtaining his Master's degree in Political Science, Homayoun moved to the United States and took a teaching position in a local college. When the tragedy of September 11th happened in the United States, following the fall of the Taliban regime in Afghanistan, I received a phone call from Homayoun, informing me that he was going back to Afghanistan to help with the reconstruction of the country. Soon after his arrival in Kabul, he played a prominent role with the new Afghan government and subsequently decided to go into private business, becoming a very successful businessman. Today he lives in Kabul.

During that time in Montpelier, there was also an Afghan ophthalmologist in Montpellier by the name of Kabir who worked at a hospital across from the university. He was married to a French woman and had three young kids. One day while he was going to his car that parked in a parking lot where we were standing, he overheard us talking in Dari. He came and introduced himself and from that day, we all became good friends with him and looked up to him for advice. After work Dr. Kabir would sometimes come and visit us at the dorm and chat. At the dorm, we had a ping pong table in the basement. Dr. Kabir liked to play ping pong and I spent hours playing with him. The dorm complex also had a couple of volleyball and basketball courts and during our free time we played sports and organized ping pong tournaments and watched television together.

Montpellier was a beautiful college town with great universities. Summers in Montpellier the weather was nice and warm and since the city was close to beautiful beaches, it would attract tourists from all over Europe. At the Montpellier University, there were a number of summer programs for foreign students; therefore, during summers, Montpellier's universities and dorms would be full of new foreign students taking either French classes or participating in study abroad programs that were offered. The center of town and specifically a place called *"Place de la Comédie"* would be full of young people sitting in outdoor cafes, with music and great ambiance all night long during the summer.

Also during summers, Uncle Hamed who still lived in Switzerland (but loved the beaches in France), along with one my cousins Tamim who lived in Germany, would come and visit us. Since we were off from school and could not go back home to visit our families, we spent our summers in Montpellier, going to the beach and having fun with our guests who occasionally would come to visit us.

My best friend Akram, and I worked hard and received our undergraduate and graduate degrees from the University of Montpellier in Electrical Engineering. We then decided to apply for the Doctorate degree. I wanted to move to Paris to complete my Doctorate and Akram moved to another city in the north of France to obtain his Doctorate degree specializing in automation. I was accepted to the University of Paris XII and my research work focused on digital image processing.

During the time I was a student in Montpellier, the situation in Afghanistan had significantly deteriorated. There were over a hundred thousand Soviet soldiers in Afghanistan fighting the Afghan "Mujahedin." Indiscriminate bombing by the Soviet Air Force had destroyed many cities and villages, killing large groups of innocent civilian Afghans. The Soviet Army had used napalm bombs banned by the United Nations, dropped hundreds of thousands of personal mines in the form of toys, killing or severely injuring young children. The Afghan communist regime had imprisoned hundreds of thousands of people, torturing and killing political prisoners and creating an extremely dangerous situation for anyone not associated with the communist regime.

When I was in my second year of college, I learned that my father had been arrested and jailed as a political prisoner.

During my stay in France, I would typically receive a letter every month from my family in Kabul. Every letter started with a short paragraph from my Baaba informing me how they were doing. I noticed that in three consecutive letters over three months, my Baaba's message had not been included in the letters. I got really worried and decided to go to the telecommunications center in Montpellier and see if they could connect me to Kabul. Telephone communications with Afghanistan were not very easy. I had to go to the telecommunication center in Montpellier and give them our home phone number, and on a good day, after several tries, I could talk to someone at home for a few minutes. The other reason I could not do that frequently -- the high cost, and as a student on a tight budget I could not afford to call home often. But Baaba's missing messages in the letters I received from home created significant fear and anxiety for me and I needed to talk to someone at home to find out why my Baaba was not writing me anymore.

I arrived at the telecommunication center and told one of the telephone operators that I needed to talk to my family in Kabul, Afghanistan. After several tries, she got me connected and I was able to hear my Mom's voice. I started crying and asked about my Baaba. She stayed calm and collected and told me to be brave. She told me that my Baaba was alive and he was not sick but had been arrested by the government to answer some questions and would be released very soon.

She also asked me to stop worrying and focus on my education and everything would be fine. The line got disconnected and I continued crying in that telephone booth. The telephone operator came to check on me and asked if everything was okay with me. I said yes and left the center.

There was nothing I could do, and knowing the savagery of the communist regime, I didn't even know if my Baaba was alive. I took the bus back to my dorm, sad and depressed, and started writing a letter to my Baaba. Then I stopped, not sure if he would even see that letter.

Baaba ended up spending more than two years in prison as a political prisoner because he had worked for the previous administration.

While studying and living in France, one of my classmates in high school named Jamal kept in touch with me. I occasionally received letters from him and wrote back to him. After completing high school, Jamal started his college education at the Kabul University School of Engineering. He loved building stuff and I knew he enjoyed so much becoming an engineer. Several months after my arrival in Montpellier, I received a letter from Jamal from Pakistan. A long letter explaining what had happened to him and his family. His father and older brother were arrested by the Afghan Secret Service agents suspecting them of supporting the Afghan resistance movement and he had to escape Afghanistan and now lived in Pakistan as a refugee.

In his letter, he mentioned that he had applied for asylum to France and if everything goes well, he might come to France. I responded back to his letter, encouraging him not to give up and offered to help him if and when he arrived in France. A couple of months later, Jamal sent me another letter stating that his asylum application is now approved and he is planning to arrive in Paris within the next three weeks. I quickly replied back and told him that I would do everything in my power to help him when he arrived. I also asked for his detailed travel itinerary and told him that I would travel from Montpellier to Paris to meet him and bring him with me to live and continue his education in Montpellier.

Three weeks later I took the night train to Paris to meet Jamal, my friend and classmate from Kabul. While waiting in the international arrival terminal, I watched passengers coming out meeting their loved ones and then finally I saw Jamal walking out. He looked much thinner than the last time I had seen him and appeared to have lost weight. I waved at him and he ran toward me. We hugged and I reassured him that he is now in a great country and everything will be just fine. We took the train from the airport to the main train station for Montpellier.

As a student, I did not have much money, and he was just a refugee kid who had just arrived from Pakistan, however, the French Embassy and the UN Refugee Agency had provided him with some funds to help him with his needs for a few months. After purchasing two train tickets for Montpellier, we boarded the train. He looked tired, but he wanted to talk. He wanted to share his horror stories of what he had witnessed back home. He needed someone who could understand his pain and I think he believed and trusted me to be that person. I started listening to his stories about how his father and brother were badly beaten in front of him and the rest of his family before they were taken away. I could see the tears in his eyes as he described his Mom and baby sisters crying when they took his father and older brother away. His family did not have any news about their whereabouts. I tried to console him as much as I could and told him to be brave and strong for his Mom and his sister. He agreed and after listening to all of his painful stories, we also talked about other topics, joked and laughed about our lives in high school, crazy teachers, and staff.

We finally arrived in Montpellier around 4 or 5 pm. I told him that he could stay in my dorm room for a few days or weeks and we would both work on a plan for his future. He agreed and thanked me. The next morning, he told me that he wanted to study engineering in one of the best French universities. I told him about the "Grands Ecoles," known for their extremely rigorous programs, but very hard to get admitted to. It required two years of studies at preparatory schools (Ecole Preparatoires), a very difficult written entrance examination, followed by an oral exam and several interviews with professors and school admission committee members. He realized the difficulties, but told me that he would like to try that route first. I knew, it would be extremely difficult for him and he needed to improve his language skills first and then study really hard. He seemed to be ready for the challenge.

The next day, I took him to an advisor in one of the preparatory schools. I told the advisor the entire story of Jamal's life and his passion to study Engineering in one of the "Grandes Ecoles." The advisor named Monsieur Petit (ironically a tall man), started to talk to Jamal, telling him how difficult it is to get admitted to one of the "Grandes Ecoles." With his broken French, Jamal told him that could do it. Instead the advisor proposed that Jamal should try to go to a trade school and since he is good in building things, a trade school would offer him a good education and a guaranty that he will find a job after graduation. Jamal looked a bit offended by the advisor's proposal and told him "no," that he would get into a great French engineering school.

Finally, the advisor agreed to enroll him to his school and needed documentation showing that he graduated from the Kabul French high school. Jamal had another two months before starting school and he started to look for a job to earn some money and also improve his language skills. He first worked at a grocery store and then at a gas station for long hours to earn more money and also keep his mind busy.

By the time school started, Jamal managed to get a room in a university dormitory and felt eager to start his education. He went to school during the days and worked at nights at the same gas station. He did struggle in school for the first few months, but as a hardworking and intelligent young man, he completed the first year of preparatory school as an above average student. By the end of the second year, he had become more comfortable and did really well.

The next big step for him was to now take the entrance exam for the Engineering School (Grandes Ecoles). He took a few weeks off from work and concentrated on getting ready for the exam. By now, I had some confidence that Jamal may have a chance in getting admitted to a great Engineering School. He finally took the entrance exam and within a few weeks received acceptance letters from a few great schools for the written part of the examination.

He then had to go through another round of oral exams and interviews to be admitted to one of these great schools. It made me really happy to see Jamal, this refugee young man, going that far. By the end of that month, Jamal completed all of his oral exams and interviews. He now had three great offers from three outstanding French Engineering schools. He decided to attend a prestigious Grande Ecole in Paris. After completing his mechanical engineering degree, he decided to continue doing research and obtained a Master's degree followed by a Doctorate degree.

8 THE FAMILY IN KABUL – ESCAPING AFGHANISTAN – MY VISIT TO PAKISTAN

During the time I lived and studied in France, the family decided they would leave Afghanistan as soon as Baaba got released from prison. Uncle Wahed decided to leave first with his wife and two daughters. He planned to escape through the borders with Pakistan and seek asylum in America.

Accompanying him would be one of his second cousins and a good friend of his who was a young judge in Kabul at that time. All three men were afraid of being arrested by the communist regime because they were not viewed as supporters of the regime. They planned to get to Pakistan first, and, once there, they would find a safe place for the rest of their families to live, then pay a the smuggler to bring their wives and children from Afghanistan.

In Afghanistan, every able male college graduate had to perform a mandatory military service for a year. After completing their military service, college graduates would automatically receive a military ID card with the title of "officer." Uncle Wahed had completed his one year of mandatory service years ago. He had received his military ID card with his military uniform photo on it.

The three men, Uncle Wahed, his second cousin and their good friend the judge had decided to escape Afghanistan through the southern borders of Pakistan. They were planning to pay a local smuggler from the Kandahar province of Afghanistan close to the borders with Pakistan to help them with their escape.

They first had to get to Kandahar.

By then, the war had spread into almost every province of Afghanistan. The Mujahedin were fighting the communist government army and the Soviets were all over Afghanistan. The road to Kandahar had become very dangerous as some parts of that road were controlled by the communist government and other parts were controlled by the Mujahedin. Uncle Wahed and his companions left Kabul by bus for Kandahar. They had to go through many road checkpoints. One of the last road checkpoints close to the city of Kandahar was controlled by the Mujahedin. The Mujahedin asked all the passengers to get out of the bus as they were looking for any communist sympathizers, spies, or government collaborators.

They started to search all the passengers. When they searched Uncle Wahed, one of the Mujahedin found the military ID card he had been given after completing his mandatory military service. That ID simply stated he had completed the military service. But the ID had a picture of Uncle Wahed in a military uniform back when he performed his mandatory military service several years before the communist regime.

Unfortunately, the level of education and literacy in Afghanistan ranked as one of the lowest in the world. The group of Mujahedin looking at that military ID photo with his uniform assumed that he was either an military officer of the communist regime or a spy for the government. They released everyone except Uncle Wahed.

They took him to a remote area and started beating him viciously, insisting that he should confess that he worked for the communist government. Once his other two companions arrived in Kandahar City, they made contact with the smuggler who was going to take them across the border to Pakistan and told him what had happened to Uncle Wahed. The smuggler knew the group of Mujahedin who held Uncle Wahed. He made contact with that group and told them that the person they had been badly beating was not a spy or a communist. He was an engineer who was simply trying to escape the country. The group of Mujahedin felt really bad and released Uncle Wahed immediately. They also promised all three men that they would provide protection for them to escape Afghanistan. Uncle Wahed needed to recover from his new injuries caused by the Mujahedin and ended up staying in Kandahar City for a few more days.

The trio finally decided to escape Afghanistan with that same group of Mujahedin.

[It should be pointed out that in English usage, during that time, Mujahedin mostly referred to the guerrilla type military organization led by the Muslim Afghan warriors in the Soviet–Afghan War, but now it often refers to other jihadist groups in various countries.]

The first day they walked all day and at dusk arrived in a village between Afghanistan and Pakistan. They spent the first night in a mosque. Uncle Wahed had difficulty sleeping that night and he would get up and look around. His friend the judge, fearing that the group of Mujahedin might suspect that they were planning an attack or something else, would pull Uncle Wahed down and force him to sleep every time he would get up.

The next day that group of Mujahedin joined another group with some pickup trucks. They had a number of unexploded bombs and rockets that they had collected in the back of their trucks where Uncle Wahed and his companions sat next to the unexploded ammunitions.

The pickup trucks used hidden dirt roads all the way to Pakistan. Uncle Wahed told me that the bumpy road and sitting next to unexploded bombs and rockets in the back of the pickup trucks made it extremely dangerous and they weren't sure if they would ever make it to Pakistan alive. Their friend, the judge at one point moved one of the unexploded rockets that pointed at him to a direction away from the truck. They later often laughed and joked about that trip in the back of that pickup truck.

Somehow by the end of the day, they arrived in Pakistan safely and said goodbye to the group of Afghan Mujahedin. They went through some very rough days in Pakistan when they arrived. They managed to contact Uncle Abdul in America, who sent them some money, and several weeks later their wives and children joined them there, after they paid a large sum of money to a group of smugglers to bring them to Pakistan.

Meanwhile, Mom tried everything possible to secure Baaba's release. The communist government had transferred him to the notorious "Pule Charkhi Prison" on the outskirts of Kabul where he no longer faced daily interrogations and torture, but experienced other forms of inhumane treatments. Mom worried about Baaba's health. A few years before his arrest, he had been diagnosed with diabetes. By bribing people at the prison, Mom could now take medication and food to Baaba on a regular basis. She would also knock on every government official's door to see if someone could help release Baaba from the prison.

In the prison, every night, the communist killers would come up with a list of prisoners who were sentenced to be executed. The executions were happening inside the prison compound and after the collapse of the communist regime mass graves with thousands of bodies in them were discovered all around that prison.

Mom kept on contacting leads that were given to her by friends and relatives, hoping that someone would finally help. One of the leads contacted a communist sympathizer who knew someone in power who could release Baaba in return for a large sum of money. Since we did not have that large sum of money, Mom ended up selling a house we owned in Kabul and gave all the money to that communist leader.

That secured Baaba's release.

He had spent more than two years in prison. Afghanistan was no longer safe for my family and in 1984, they prepared to leave for Pakistan. They paid another smuggler a large sum of money. He took them across the border to Pakistan and they all joined Uncle Wahed and his family. They had left everything they owned behind. In Pakistan, they were no longer living under the daily terror of an oppressive regime. Baaba had some savings he brought with him, but not enough to allow them to live and support the family for a long period of time. They needed to quickly apply for asylum to America. Once again, Uncle Abdul became instrumental in helping in sponsoring everyone and helping them get all the required documents they needed to immigrate to the United States.

In the summer of 1984, when my family still lived as refugees in Pakistan, I decided to visit them from France. My French government scholarship allowed me a paid yearly trip to visit my family, and since my family did not live in Afghanistan anymore, they were kind enough to allow me to travel to Pakistan and visit them. Since I held a Service Passport issued by the Afghan Ministry of Foreign Affairs, people not knowing the background of how I obtained that passport may have assumed I was a communist sympathizer traveling on a Service Passport issued by the Afghan communist government.

That is exactly what happened when I approached the Pakistani Embassy in Paris.

In late June of 1984, I left Montpellier on a night train that arrived in the morning in Paris. I went to the Pakistani Embassy and applied for a visa to visit my family in Pakistan. I told them the entire story of what had happened to my Baaba and the rest of my family. But once they saw my blue Service Passport, they started questioning me about how a student like me, claiming that his family had escaped to Pakistan, was able to travel to France with a Service Passport. I tried to explain everything, but they did not believe me and refused to issue a visa for me to visit my family in Pakistan. Not sure what else I could do, I went to see some friends who lived in Paris and asked them if they knew anyone who could help.

One of the Afghan young men I did not personally know well, mentioned that he knew a Pakistani young man who had been in one of the refugee centers in Paris who might know some lower-level people at the Pakistan Embassy. I asked for his name and address, as I wanted to meet him as soon as possible to see if he could help. I did not want all my summer vacation spent working on acquiring the visa; however I wanted to visit my family in Pakistan really badly. I took the Metro to see this Pakistani young man. He lived in another suburb of Paris, a fairly decent refugee center for new arrivals. Once inside the center, I asked a few Afghan young men where I could locate the person I sought. They all seemed to know this person and I also learned that he had come to France as an Afghan refugee and not as a Pakistani, as he spoke fluent Pashtu, one of the two official languages of Afghanistan.

They all warned me not to mention the word "Pakistani" as he did not want the French authorities to know that he was actually from the Peshawar region of Pakistan close to the border with Afghanistan. I finally found him. His real name was Mohammad, but everyone called him Momo.

He was in his early 20s, a short and chubby young man, and very friendly. He mainly spoke Pashtu. I started to tell him about my problem and wanted to know if he knew someone who could help.

Momo seemed very nervous at first, as he did not know me and also did not want to be known as a Pakistani. I quickly put him at ease, telling him that I had many good friends in that center and one of my closest friends in Montpellier, was Tor, had spent four months in the same refugee center as he. When I mentioned Tor's name, he quickly asked a few more questions, making sure that we were talking about the same Tor. He also knew Tor, as he had helped Momo when he first arrived at the center. After trying to build some trust, he said he knew someone who knew a cook at the Pakistani Embassy and he wasn't sure if he would be able to help, but he agreed to go with me and meet his friend. Momo and I took the Metro to meet his friend. He was working in a restaurant not too far from the center. After a quick introduction, his friend agreed to help and go with us to the Pakistani Embassy in the morning and talk to his friend to see if he had any way of helping me get a visa. I spent another night in Paris, renting a room in a dorm reserved for foreign students who were in transit in Paris.

The next morning, we all met in front of the Pakistani Embassy and Momo asked me to give some cash to his friends as it was customary in Pakistan to use cash when asking someone to do a favor. I had a 100 Francs in my wallet and gave it to Momo and he gave it to his friends. They took my passport and asked me to wait outside of the embassy. Momo and I waited there for more than two hours. We finally saw Momo's friend come out of the embassy, not looking too happy, walking towards us. He shook his head in a disappointed gesture and told us that they rejected my application for a visa. Simply put, the Pakistani cook who worked inside the embassy could not help. Obviously disappointed, I still thanked them for trying, took my passport and left.

I walked along the streets of Paris for at least an hour thinking about what else I could do to obtain a visa to Pakistan. I literally got mad at myself for a few minutes and then decided to go back inside the Pakistani Embassy and ask to meet a high-ranking official and explain that I was not a communist sympathizer, that my entire family had suffered and been victimized by the communist regime in Afghanistan; and that my entire family lived now in Pakistan as refugees and that my Service Passport could not in any way be an indication that I am associated with the puppet regime of Kabul. I soon realized that I had actually told that entire story the first time when I had applied for a visa. But the Pakistani official working in the visa section of the embassy still did not believe me. After some more thinking, I was even more determined to find another way to obtain a visa and visit my family in Pakistan.

I spent another night in Paris thinking about my next move. My Mom had a cousin who had been working for the United Nations for a long time. He had been educated in the United States and had a Ph.D. in Chemistry. When I was a child in Afghanistan, at one point he had even become the Vice Minister of Education in Afghanistan under King Zaher Shah's rule. He now lived with his wife and children in Paris, working as Director in the Education Sector for the United Nations Educational, Scientific, and Cultural Organization (UNESCO).

They had invited me to their house for dinner once a couple of years ago. His wife was a sweet lady and wanted me to stay in touch with them while I was in France and visit them on a regular basis. But unfortunately that dinner was the only time I had been to their house. In the morning, I decided to call my Mom's cousin who worked at UNESCO.

I had his office phone number and was able to connect with him. He was happy to hear from me and after asking about his wife and children, I gave him an update about what had happened to my family and told him that they were now refugees in Pakistan. I also explained that I had a major problem getting a visa with my Service Passport from the Pakistani Embassy. Since he was considered a diplomat and had the same status as other foreign diplomats in Paris, he knew a large number of high-ranking officials who worked at the embassies in Paris.

He told me that he was going to help me and also mentioned that his wife and kids were in London visiting his son who was a student there. He asked me to meet him after work at the Metro station close to the UNESCO building and we would go have dinner and I could spend the night at his house. Then in morning he would go with me to the Pakistani Embassy to see what he could do. I thanked him and around 5:00 pm, I went to the Metro station where we planned to meet. After several minutes, I saw him walking toward me. He was a classy man, always well-dressed and charismatic. He hugged me and told me that I had changed and grown so much since the last time he had seen me about two years earlier. We took the Metro to his house in an upscale neighborhood of Paris. He lived in a large two-story apartment overlooking the Seine River. After we arrived, we went into his living room, and after drinking a glass of water, he asked me to go out to eat dinner.

We walked to a local restaurant in his neighborhood. The food tasted great and seemed expensive. After dinner, we walked in a park close to his house and we talked. I told him about my Baaba spending two years in prison, because he was part of the old administration and all the sagas about the family's escape from Afghanistan. He was a knowledgeable person but talked cautiously, careful not to take a clear political position, but he clearly felt absolutely horrified by what was going on in Afghanistan.

It was getting late and we decided to head back to his place. In the morning, we both woke up around the same time; I helped him fix a quick breakfast in his kitchen and after breakfast we headed out. He did not tell me that he knew people in the Pakistani Embassy; all he said was:

"Let's go see what we could do."

I knew exactly which Metro line to take to the Pakistani Embassy. When we arrived at the embassy, he introduced himself, making sure that they understood that he was a high-ranking United Nations official working at the UNESCO organization in Paris and said that he was there to meet with the General Counsel. The embassy staff we talked to called someone inside the embassy and we were allowed to go inside the building. After entering the building, another person guided us to the General Counsel's office. When the Pakistani General Counsel saw my Mom's cousin, he got up and walked toward us, shook his hand, and greeted him warmly. He also said hello to me and shook my hand. By then, I realized that they knew each other really well. They started talking about family, weather and other unofficial topics first. My Mom's cousin then explained my situation and told him that he needed his help.

The General Counsel picked up his phone and called someone to come to his office. Once that person was in his office, he spoke to him in Urdu, took my passport, and left the office quickly. Within 10 minutes, he was back in the office with my passport. He handed me the passport and told me that they had issued a three-month tourist visa for now and if that wasn't enough time, they could extend it even more. I thanked the man and the General Counsel and we left the embassy. Outside, my Mom's cousin gave me a hug and wished me a safe trip, asking me to make sure I said hello to everyone from him once I arrived in Pakistan.

Happy and excited, I went straight to the foreign student office in Paris and they called their travel agency and booked my flight to Pakistan. I could not wait to go and see my family. My plane ticket was booked for the end of that week.

I was ready for my flight to leave Paris for Pakistan. Before my departure, I managed to communicate the details of my trip to the family in Pakistan on a quick phone call. My plane left Paris for Karachi, one of the largest cities in Pakistan. I then had to spend one night in Karachi in a hotel before the next leg of my flight from Karachi to Islamabad. The flight from Paris to Karachi had been long and exhausting, as I could not sleep in the Air France 747 Jumbo Jet. After 10 hours in the air, we landed in Karachi. It was nighttime there. Once arriving at the airport and going through immigration and customs, I had to go to a designated area outside of the airport to catch a hotel shuttle.

Karachi is the most populous city in Pakistan and one of the largest cities in the world. The population: 16 million when I visited, more than 24 million today. Since it was summer, even at night the weather was very hot and humid. As Karachi serves as a major transport hub and is home to two of Pakistan's largest seaports, one can imagine how crowded that city must be. Once outside, I got mobbed by a group of people trying to carry my luggage to earn a few dollars. Some spoke to me in Urdu. Others talked to me in Pashtu or English, not knowing where I was from. I did not let anyone carry my luggage and walked out very firmly toward the hotel shuttle.

I arrived at the hotel and quickly went through registration. They assigned me a room and I could not wait to get to bed and sleep. I slept for several hours and woke up very early in the morning. I took a shower, changed and went to the restaurant of the hotel to have breakfast. My flight from Karachi to Islamabad was scheduled for around 9:00 a.m. local time. I arrived at the airport early enough to check my luggage and got to the assigned gate for my flight. My flight departed from Karachi on time and after a brief stop in Lahore, I arrived in Islamabad, located next to another large city called Rawalpindi. Islamabad, along with the Rawalpindi metropolitan area, forms the third largest area in Pakistan with a population exceeding five million.

At first, my family had lived in Islamabad for a few weeks and since summers are extremely hot, humid and brutal there, they had wanted to see if they could live in a place with a cooler climate. They were told about Murree, a small city not too far from Islamabad, with a rich history. Murree was founded in 1851 and it was the summer headquarters of the colonial Punjab government during the British occupation of India. Murree became a popular tourist station for the British within British India, and several prominent Englishmen were born there. Since the Independence of Pakistan in 1947, Murree had retained its position as a popular cooler resort with an elevation of 7,500 feet, noted for its pleasant summers. A large number of tourists visited the town from the Islamabad-Rawalpindi area. The town also served as a transit point for tourists visiting Kashmir and Abbottabad, where Osama Bin Laden was hiding. Many wealthy Pakistanis owned a summer retreat in the resort town of Murree. In Murree, finding a rental home for an Afghan refugee family was not easy, but with Uncle Abdul's help, the family managed to rent a modest home at the entrance of Murree and stayed there until they left for America.

When my plane landed, I could not wait to get out of the airplane and see my loved ones. As soon as I left the plane, I walked really quickly, almost running to get my luggage. Once I retrieved my luggage, I walked out where passengers were greeted by their families and loved ones. From a distance, I could see my Baaba, my Mom, and Uncle Wahed. I was tired but overjoyed to see the faces I had missed so dearly for so long. I ran toward them, threw myself into their arms, and started hugging them. I was also crying from happiness, full of emotions and pain to see my dear Baaba who

151

had been tortured and imprisoned for over two years, to see my Mom, who had endured so much hardship while my Baaba was in prison, and to see Uncle Wahed alive after everything he had gone through.

We were all teary-eyed while continuing to kiss and hug each other. Then wiping our tears, my Baaba said we needed to get going, as we had to go to the Murree bus station and catch a bus home. We soon walked out of the airport and walked for 10 to 15 minutes to our bus station. Islamabad was hot and humid and I was all wet in sweat just walking for a short distance. We all got on the bus and after my Baaba paid the driver, we sat in the same section of the bus close to my Mom and Baaba. I continued to look at their faces and realized that in just a few years, how much older they looked. My Baaba had his arms around me while I was sitting next to him and it felt so good. I was in heaven to see my parents alive and could not wait to get home to see the rest of the family. On the way to Murree, I asked Baaba about prison and his interrogations, but he did not want to share painful memories of being tortured with me.

He was a strong man and he told me this saying from a wise man:

"If one makes it going through rough times, he will be much stronger."

He told me that he was just fine and much stronger and smiled at me.

I then asked Mom how she was doing and how did she cope with so much hardship.

Mom, as the rock of the family, laughed and said, "Now that you are here, everything is just fine and we could not be happier." Then I looked at Uncle Wahed who was sitting next to Mom; he looked a bit frail as he still was dealing with health issues from the rocket attack, but as always, he had a smile on his face and told me that he was happy to see his best friend again.

We finally arrived in Murree and my Baaba called on the bus driver to stop the vehicle. Murree, with its winding roads, reminded me of Afghanistan and the road from Kabul to Mazar-i-Sharif, the Salang Pass and Hindukush Mountains. The bus stopped and we all got out. My Baaba wanted to carry my luggage and I did not allow him to do that. He took my smaller bag as we walked toward the small home they had rented there. Within five minutes, we arrived at the door of the house and everyone was waiting for us; I saw Grandpa Baaba Jaan, Grandma Bobo Jaan, my sisters, Flora and Hanna, my baby brother and baby sister Abe and Mina, my Aunt Khala Jaan and her husband and Uncle Wahed's wife and their young daughters.

I was still very emotional seeing them all. I had finally arrived home. It was lunchtime and my Aunt Khala Jaan had prepared lunch and like the old days, we all sat around on the floor while they brought lunch. I was hungry by now and sharing a meal with my family again was so special. I really enjoyed the delicious meal with my family after so many years. After lunch, I felt so happy to be there encircled by the loved ones who endured so much and I was thrilled they were all alive. They started sharing stories about Kabul, and how dangerous it had become. They talked about close relatives who were still in prison and the unlucky ones who were killed by the communist Secret Service agents. I could see through their eyes, the scary experiences, the close encounters with death, and the risks they had to take to escape Afghanistan, leaving everything behind. Mom soon realized how exhausted I was, and she told me to lie down on a small mattress on the floor. I fell asleep on that mattress for a while and Mom put a blanket on top of me.

I woke up after a couple of hours and Baaba wanted to take me to the Bazaar in Murree and show me around. Murree is a mountainous area with gorgeous hilltops. The streets were muddy and narrow, people walking everywhere, on sidewalks or just in the middle of the roads. The weather seemed much nicer than in Islamabad. Baaba had made many friends, even without knowing any Urdu. I believe he had that unique gift and trait to make friends everywhere quickly. When we walked through the Bazaar, most shopkeepers knew my Baaba and would say "Hi" to him. My younger brother Abe, who must have been five at that time, also came with us. The road from our house went up through the Bazaar.

I felt like I was in a dream; I had never imagined meeting my own family in a place like this. Abe had quickly picked up some Urdu words and I noticed that he understood what people were talking about -- an amazing scene being there walking with my Baaba and younger brother in this new country that we knew so little about. In the days and weeks that followed, I learned more about what had happened with my family during the years I had been away. I devoured the home cooked meals that I missed so dearly. I went to the Friday Prayers with Baaba, Granpa Baaba Jaan and Uncle Wahed and also enjoyed the spicy food consumed in Pakistan.

My month-long stay in Murree passed really quickly and then I prepared to return to France where I would live the fairly comfortable student life, leaving the rest of the family in Pakistan with an uncertain future. Comforting to me at that time -- the fact that they were no longer in danger and no longer lived under constant terror. The day of my departure, we left really early in the morning, taking the bus from Murree to Islamabad. Mom, Baaba and Uncle Wahed accompanied me. Before getting on the bus, I said my good byes to everyone, hugging and kissing them; again everyone cried not knowing when we would see each other again. I left a bit sad, but had to go, as my planned trip had come to an end.

We arrived in Islamabad in the morning and took a taxi to the international airport. My flight back to France would again go through Karachi, so the first leg of the flight from Islamabad to Karachi was on an internal Pakistani airline. After an hour of delay, my flight was ready to board. I hugged and kissed Mom, Baaba and Uncle Wahed and boarded my flight. I arrived in Karachi early in the afternoon and my flight from Karachi to Paris with Air France was scheduled for later that evening. I tried to pass some time by reading a book I had with me. Then a couple of hours before my scheduled flight, I went to the Air France ticket counter, checked my bag and obtained my boarding pass. In my carryon luggage, my Mom had packed some food for me.

My friends in France had asked to me bring a unique cantaloupe that can only be found in north of Afghanistan. This cantaloupe is very sweet, juicy and known all over the region. Afghans were bringing all sorts of fresh fruits to sell in Pakistan, including that famous cantaloupe. That morning Baaba had bought me a large cantaloupe from Islamabad and my plan was to take it with me as part of my carryon items inside the airplane. About an hour and half before my flight, I lined up with the other passengers to go through passport checkpoints, thinking it would be a fairly routine process and I would soon be boarding my plane.

But when I arrived at the passport checkpoint, a Pakistani officer looked surprised at my passport; he seemed surprised to see a young man like me with a Service Passport typically reserved for government officials. He looked through pages of my passport and saw that I had obtained a valid tourist visa for my stay in Pakistan. He then asked me a few more questions about my visit, which I answered. He then asked me where my Exit Permit was. I did not know what he meant and told him all I had was a valid visa to visit my family and I was just going back to where I came from. I also explained to him that I was an Afghan student in France.

Without any other word, he threw my Afghan Passport back at me and told me that I could not leave the country without an Exit Permit and he ordered an airport worker to bring my checked luggage back from the airplane to me. I begged him to let me leave, saying that I did not know how to obtain an Exit Permit. Also I did not have enough money to buy another plane ticket to return to Islamabad to ask my family to help. The officer was rude and wasn't even paying attention to what I was saying and asked me to step aside and let the other passengers go.

It was an ironic if not comical scene -- I held a small carryon bag in one hand and a big cantaloupe in the other.

Within 10 minutes, I saw an airport employee coming towards me with my checked luggage. By then I felt fairly certain that they would not allow me to board my flight. I ran to the Air France ticket counter and asked for their help, but unfortunately they could do nothing, as passport control was not something they were able to help me with. Helpless, in this large airport in one of the largest cities of Pakistan, I was desperately looking for someone to help me. I did not speak the language; my English was far from perfect, and I felt stuck there. Mentally and physically exhausted, I went to a corner of the airport and watched my flight take off. Sad and disappointed, I needed to collect myself and come up with a plan. I first wanted to unload some of the items I was carrying with me, especially the cantaloupe (sorry friends) and the other food items my Mom had packed for me. I went outside of the main terminal and saw a couple of Pakistani poor people begging for money. I donated my cantaloupe and the food that I had in my carryon bag. I went back inside the terminal and my only plan was to somehow go back to Islamabad, then take the bus to Murree and ask my Baaba for help.

I would later realize the amount of corruption and bribery in Pakistan. Most people in a position of power in Pakistan, even today, like that passport officer who did not allow me to board my flight, were looking to supplement their regular income by taking bribe money from innocent people.

I did not know that.

Otherwise, I would have probably handed that officer a few hundred dollars and I am sure he would have allowed me to leave Pakistan. I first counted how much money I had on me and I believe it was less than $500. I then went to the Pakistani Airlines ticket counter to get some information on the cost of flights back to Islamabad from Karachi. The next flight was going to leave in a couple of hours and it looked like I had enough money to pay for a one-way ticket. I purchased it and flew back to Islamabad. I arrived late at night and had enough money left to pay for my bus trip to Murree.

I arrived at the home my family had rented in Murree past midnight. I knocked on the door a few times, assuming that everyone was sleeping, and heard someone coming to the door. Uncle Wahed asked in Urdu who was behind the door this late waking them up. I quietly told him that it was me. Shocked, he quickly opened the door. I entered the house and told him the whole saga of my adventure in Karachi at the airport. He smiled and told me that by handing the official a few dollars I could have resolved the issue, but reassured me that they would take care of everything in the morning. He went and woke up my Mom and Baaba. They were both happy to see me again and said they were sorry I had gone through so much trouble. Mom prepared a spot on the floor for me to sleep that night. In the morning, everyone said they had assumed that my next call would be from France when I landed there. They were surprised to find me sleeping on the floor of the house in Murree.

The next day, Baaba and I took the bus to Islamabad to meet an Afghan friend who lived there and he showed us where to obtain that Exit Permit. We went to an official building and Baaba gave some money to a Pakistani official working there along with my passport and within five minutes he handed us a small piece of paper that represented the Exit

Permit from Pakistan. Since I did not have enough money to purchase another plane ticket from Islamabad to Karachi, Baaba went to a local travel agency and purchased my plane ticket to Karachi and also rescheduled my flight with Air France. We went back to Murree and spent another night with the family. This time, I asked Mom to please not pack me any food as it was still very hot and also decided not to take that famous Afghan cantaloupe for my friends.

We went through the same routine as the last time, and I finally arrived in Karachi for the second time in a week. After checking my bag and getting my boarding pass from the Air France ticket counter, I waited in line to go through the passport checkpoint at the airport. This time I purposefully put the Exit Permit in my pocket and was only going to hand it to the officer when the officer asked for it. When I handed my passport to a different passport officer than the last time, he looked at my valid passport and stamped my passport and let me go without asking for that Exit Permit. I was disappointed but happy to leave Pakistan and hoped to never go back there again.

I arrived in Paris the next day in the morning, and one of the first things I did was to call the family back in Murree to tell them that I had arrived safely in Paris. Since they did not have a telephone in their home, they had given me the phone number of their landlord who lived next door and he gave the message to my family. I had enough money for a train ticket to Montpellier and decided to go straight there.

With the help of Uncle Abdul from America, the family started the process of applying for asylum to the United States. By now Uncle Abdul had moved to the East Coast. After several months of waiting in Pakistan, in 1985 the family finally immigrated to the United States.

9 PARIS, THE CITY OF LIGHTS – COMPLETING MY DOCTORATE DEGREE

In 1987, after completing my *Diplome d'Etude Approfondie or DEA*, (equivalent to a Master's degree) in Montpellier I was admitted to the University of Paris XII to work toward a Ph.D. I had a very dear friend in Paris, Tawab, a student at the same university where I would do research for my Doctorate. I first lived in a dorm where Tawab lived and then moved into an apartment in a suburb of Paris called Creteil. Up to that point, I had traveled through Paris, but never lived there. The city is vibrant, classy and multidimensional, with every arrondissement known for something specific, be it modern or historical (Paris is divided into 20 such administrative districts).

The Metro system is probably one of the best in Europe. There is no need to own a car if one lives and works in Paris or the suburbs. One place I especially liked near the famous University of Sorbonne was the *"Quartier Latin"* or Latin Quarter, full of affordable restaurants and young people frequenting the cafés and bars. At nights, Paris had a different magic that is hard to find in any other cities across Europe or even around the world. The wide Champs Elyse Boulevard literally hums with cars and sidewalks full of people either walking or sitting outside. Lights glitter everywhere, different colors of lights that bring more vibrancy to the overall atmosphere. Known as a city of arts and museums, without exaggeration, one could spend weeks visiting all the museums and art galleries. While walking on the streets of Paris, one notices a high level of sophistication and beauty when it comes to fashion. The Seine River flowing through the heart of the city adds another dimension to the beauty of this magical place. I truly loved walking the streets of Paris and enjoying everything this magnificent city had to offer.

I lived in the modest suburb of Creteil close to my university. I shared a room in an apartment with three other students. The area was full of North African immigrants and was a relatively safe area. My research work at the university was fascinating. I performed research in digital image processing and motion tracking. The head of the department, Mr. Lefranc, was a stylish French professor, always dressed impeccably, who cared about all of his staff and made sure that the department had the latest and greatest technologies for our work. All researchers and professors were friendly and I felt comfortable working in that type of an environment.

My research work was going well and, since digital image processing required a fair amount of computer programming, I taught myself new computer programming languages and quickly learned advanced techniques to manipulate complex graphics forms on a computer monitor. I also published research papers in journals, and then traveled to scientific conferences to make presentations of my work. After about three years of research, I was ready to submit my work to the head of the department to meet the requirements of my Doctorate degree. Mr. Lefranc selected a committee of respected professors and researchers to read my doctoral dissertation and then scheduled a date for my Doctoral Defense.

I was allowed to invite friends and family the day of my defense and I asked all of my friends to be there that day. I also wanted to invite Mademoiselle Chaumet, the math professor who helped me during my first year in France. Mademoiselle Chaumet not only helped me succeed that first year, but she also made me believe that with hard work and dedication I could become more successful. In some ways I owed her that Doctorate degree. I called the school in Bordeaux where Mademoiselle Chaumet taught. They told me that she had retired several years earlier and they did not have her contact information. I looked through the phone books at the telecommunications center and called a few numbers, but unfortunately I could not find her. I was disappointed that Mademoiselle Chaumet was not there that day; I am sure she would have been proud of me. *Merci Beaucoup, Mademoiselle Chaumet!*

The day of defense of my research work for my Doctorate degree, I woke up early and arrived at the university and went straight to the large auditorium where I was going to present my research work to the Defense Committee. I had prepared a number of transparencies for a large screen projector to use for my presentation. An hour later, I saw Monsieur Lefranc enter the room; he asked me if I was ready. I responded with confidence that yes, I was ready and thanked him for all of his support. All Doctorate Defense Committee members arrived one by one and took their seats. All of my other friends sat in the audience section of the auditorium. Monsieur Lefranc introduced me and quickly talked about my research work and then it was my turn. I was a bit nervous, but ready. I did a good job presenting my research work to the committee and answered all of their questions. The committee went into another room to deliberate. Within 30 minutes, Monsieur Lefranc entered the auditorium with the all members of the

Defense Committee and asked everyone to have a seat. The President of the Defense Committee got up and started to congratulate me for my research work and told me that the committee decided to award me my Doctorate degree with the highest honors. I thanked the President of the Defense Committee and all the members, and also thanked Monsieur Lefranc and the university for all of their support. My friends hugged me and congratulated me.

I had finished school at last.

After completing my education in France, I really wanted to be reunited with the rest of the family in the United States. I had already applied and received my green card and was ready to start living my American dream.

I ended up spending nine and half years in France. I loved France and its people, as it had become a second home country to me, allowing me to pursue any dreams of furthering my education, giving me the opportunity to advance as far as I could and obtain a Doctorate degree. France is a beautiful country with amazing food and wonderful people. I have many great memories from my time in France and made many great friends with whom I still remain in contact. Being a young student in Europe allowed me to travel to many other Western European countries on public transportation and train systems that were among the best in world.

When I was a student in Montpellier one summer, I decided with a couple of my good friends to purchase a student train pass to travel and visit some of the other European countries. The student train pass was not expensive and allowed students unlimited travel from the end of June to the end of August to any Western European country. We packed our small backpacks and left Montpellier on a warm July morning. We ended up visiting Germany, England, Italy, Spain and Belgium, sleeping in inexpensive youth hostels, and meeting many young men and women from countries around the world. It was one my best summers in Europe. I found it fascinating to learn more about these small European countries, each with a different language, unique culture, diverse foods, and amazing people.

I also traveled when I was performing research for my Doctorate degree, going to conferences that had accepted one of my research papers, and I would often make a presentation describing my research work. One of those conferences was organized in Oulu, Finland. I had never been to a Scandinavian country and my department approved my trip to Oulu. I ended up going to Finland with one of my research advisers and another Ph.D. student who was originally from Morocco. The adviser who decided to go with us was a young French professor, who looked like a graduate student and was a smart and fun person. The three of us planned to leave on a Friday before the conference and spend that weekend in Helsinki, Finland. It was summertime and we all thought this would be a great opportunity for us to visit this famous and beautiful city that had hosted the 1952 Summer Olympic Games. We decided not to reserve a hotel room ahead of time. Our plan was to take public transportation from the Helsinki airport when we arrived, go downtown, and look for a low-cost place to spend the weekend. We left Paris on an evening flight and arrived in Helsinki at night. From the airport we took a bus to the middle of the downtown area.

When we arrived, a large organized concert was going on with hundreds of people dancing and listening to music. We joined the party and enjoyed the festive atmosphere there. At the end of the concert, we started to ask people for information on low-cost hotels. It was a Friday night, a vibrant night in Helsinki, and most young people were drinking, some heavily. One of the young men we talked to told us in fluent English that he knew of a nice place we could spend the night. All excited, we asked for directions, and the next thing we knew he had hailed a cab and told us he would take us there. He sat in the front seat of this small taxi and told the driver something in Finnish. We were hoping to be at our hotel within the next 5 or 10 minutes.

But after about 15 minutes, we started to get worried and communicated with each other in French. We asked the young man about the location of the hotel and he kept saying, "It's not too far." After about 25 to 30 minutes, we arrived in what appeared to be a fairly large apartment complex. We got out of the car and the young Finnish man told us that we had arrived at our destination. We realized that we were not going to spend our night in a low-cost hotel and were thinking that he must have an empty apartment and would charge us some money for spending the night there. After the taxi left, he told us that we would be spending the night in his apartment.

Then we really got worried. We had no idea who he was, having just met him a half an hour ago in a new city and a new country. Our young adviser told the two of us, that no matter what, all three of us had to stay together in the same room that night. Since we did not have any other viable options and none of us spoke Finnish, we decided to take the risk and spend the night at this stranger's apartment. He had a modest apartment, not too fancy, and decently furnished. When we got inside the apartment, we told him that all three of us would sleep in the same room to make sure we didn't create too much of a headache for him. He did not object, showed us a small bedroom with a bed, and brought us a couple of sleeping bags. None of us slept well and could not wait for the morning to arrive so we could ask him to call for a cab and leave.

Early in the morning, we heard the doorbell ring and heard a female voice. We were still not sure what was going to happen to us. Within an hour, we heard a knock on our bedroom door. Our adviser opened the door and the young Finnish man told him that breakfast was ready, while introducing his girlfriend to us. Seeing another person in the apartment was a bit more reassuring, knowing that we were no longer alone with this man. We all got up and went to the kitchen where he had made some coffee with toast. As both the young man and his girlfriend spoke English, and we all knew enough English to maintain simple conversations. We quickly learned that he was just a nice young man who wanted to help us that night. We were amazed by his hospitality and also a bit surprised about how careless he was to invite three strangers to spend the night in his apartment. In any case, we thanked him for his kindness and told him that we were ready to leave, as we were planning to visit the city of Helsinki.

He offered to drive us downtown. He told us that since he knew he was going to drink at the concert, he had left his car in the garage of his apartment. We now felt much more comfortable with him and accepted his offer to take us back downtown. He not only took us back downtown, but spent a good part of the day showing us major historical and artistic areas of Helsinki. Before he left, we thanked him for his kindness and told him that we were a bit scared when he took us to his apartment. He started laughing about that. He still offered us another night at his place, but we kindly declined, as we wanted to stay downtown and found a nice place to spend the next night there. After having a good time in Helsinki, we took another flight to Oulu to attend the research conference.

Oulu is a city in the northern region of Finland and was considered one of Europe's "living labs," as people were willing to experiment with new technologies such as Near-Field Communication or NFC tags and the wide use of computers and computing devices, the Internet, mobile networks connecting appliances and other devices. Another fun fact that I discovered in Finland is that because of its location on earth, the year is divided in half with six months of daytime and six months of nighttime.

10 IMMIGRATING TO THE LAND OF OPPORTUNITY: AMERICA

I left France for good in the summer of 1990 and immigrated to the United States to reunite with my family. Everyone from our family by then lived on the East Coast, because Uncle Abdul worked there as a medical doctor and had helped the family settle in.

My Baaba, who did not speak English, started to do all kinds of odd jobs, from washing dishes to delivering food, to cleaning, etc. He was no longer a young man but always valued hard work and even though he had held many high ranking administrative positions in Afghanistan (Provincial Governor), he was not ashamed of working and starting from scratch in a new country where everything was different, from language to people, to cars, to roads, etc. Despite missing his homeland, Baaba loved America. Even with his limited knowledge of the English language, he made many friends from many different backgrounds. He enjoyed and valued the diversity of the people of the United States.

One of Baaba's good friends was a nice gentleman named Mike, who was in his early 30s. Mike was an American businessman from

Pennsylvania and Baaba was introduced to him through one of the local churches helping new refugees find jobs. Mike had offered Baaba a job that did not require much knowledge of the English language. During that time, Mike learned more about Baaba's past, our family and what we had endured. He slowly became a really good family friend. Mike of Irish origins with his lovely wife, Karen, had four young children of their own. At the same time they were foster parents to several more children as well. Despite their hectic and busy lifestyle, Mike and Karen took great care of all the children in their home. He called Baaba his friend and helped him in any way he could.

When I arrived to the United States, I knew just enough English to at least communicate, but my English was not good enough to apply for a teaching position at a college or university. So I decided to take part-time, hourly-paid sales jobs at a department store, then worked as a cashier in a fried chicken fast-food restaurant, and worked at night cleaning an office building. When applying for these temporary jobs, I hid the fact that I was highly educated. I just wanted to practice my English and earn some money in the process.

I remember when working at the fried chicken restaurant for a few weeks as a cashier, I became the employee of the month and the manager wanted to take a picture of me for a plaque to hang on one of the walls of the restaurant. I begged the manager not to do that and after several requests he finally agreed. While doing these odd jobs, I was also sending my resume and job applications to companies and university departments that needed someone with my educational background. I must have sent hundreds of resumes. I would occasionally be called for an interview, but after a few months, I was still looking for a "real" job.

Our new family friend, Mike, already knew that I had studied in France. When I arrived in the United States, I first met Mike at our house one evening when he came for a visit. He was a tall gentleman, kind, calm, generous with a great smile and addictive laughter. He told me that he would help me find a "real" job and gave me hope that I would have a bright future in the United States. Sometimes on weekends, Mike would make the two-hour drive to our home to pick up Baaba, Abe, Mina and me and take us along with all of his children to visit great places on the East Coast. We always enjoyed his company and we all consider Mike, Karen and the kids as members of our extended family in America. I will never forget the days Mike would take time from his extremely busy schedule and take me to visit technology companies that would be a good fit for my educational background, exploring potential job opportunities.

Baaba continued to work until he had a brain hemorrhage. I lived in Texas during that time and rushed to see him the day after he had the stroke. Heartbroken, I arrived at the hospital and went straight to seen him. Mom, my brother Emile and some other close relatives were in his room. Unconscious, Baaba laid on a hospital bed after surgery. I tried to call him and tell him that I was there and I loved him. I held his hand close to my heart and then kiss it while crying. Unfortunately, he did not recover and a week later passed away. Losing Baaba after everything he had endured proved to be extremely painful for all of us. I still miss his smiling face, his charming personality, his kind and generous nature.

Mike was really sad when Baaba passed away and he published a thoughtful article in a local newspaper about him and our family. I know that Baaba loved Mike like a younger brother and he was always happy to see him. Mike and Karen still live in Pennsylvania, and we are still in touch with them. They always make sure to visit our family when they can.

I continued my temporary jobs for many months. One evening before going to my restaurant job, I received a phone call from Dr. Jim Flanagan, the head of research department at a large research university on the East Coast. He told me that he had received a copy of my resume and was interested in talking to me. I was excited, thanked him for the call, and arranged to meet with him the next day. Wearing a nice suit I had brought with me from France and a nice winter coat, as it was very cold that winter, I drove to the university. The drive was more than an hour and a half but I arrived there on time.

I entered the designated building, asked for the office of Dr. Jim Flanagan, introduced myself to his secretary, and told her that I had an appointment with Dr. Flanagan. She politely asked me to have a seat and went into Dr. Flanagan's office. Within a minute or two, the secretary came out with a tall skinny gentleman with reddish hair and a receding hairline, who she introduced as Jim Flanagan. I introduced myself and he invited me into his office. I took my winter coat off before having a seat and Dr. Flanagan took my coat and hung it neatly on a coat hanger in the corner of his office. We both sat down and Dr. Flanagan started to talk about himself, briefly telling me that he recently retired from AT&T Bell Labs, where he was the head of the Signal Processing Lab and joined the university to create a Multimedia Research lab.

He then asked me about my background and the type of research I had done. I told him about my research work in digital image processing and motion tracking, which he found very interesting. While in France doing research, I had heard of a Dr. Jim Flanagan who was considered the father of modern Voice and Speech Processing. Dr. Flanagan mentioned that his research focus had mainly been voice processing, voice coding and voice synthesis. For his new research lab, he needed a few researchers to work on voice/speech and video coding. He asked me if I was interested in considering a Post-Doctoral Research position or a Research Professor position in video coding/compression and I gladly said yes. He then asked me when I could start and I told him I was available as soon as he would like me to start.

Dr. Jim Flanagan had just offered me my first "real" job in the United States.

Although I had not worked on video coding or video compression before, I did have the necessary skills and understanding to do research in that field. We jointly decided on a start date for me to officially become part of his new research team. Before leaving his office, he asked me to talk to another Post-Doctoral researcher fellow that he had just hired to get additional information on the program. I thanked him for his trust and kindness and left his office.

His secretary introduced me to the other Post-Doctoral research fellow that Dr. Flanagan wanted me to talk to. We both walked into a small conference room and started introducing ourselves. The researcher's name was Mike, and he asked me if I had known Dr. Flanagan. I said no and told him that I had only known one famous Dr. Flanagan who was considered the father of speech processing. With a big smile, Mike told him that I had just met that famous Dr. Flanagan. I was a bit shocked that I was in the presence of one the most famous engineers and scientists in the world.

Despite being so well-known, highly respected, and someone who had won so many scientific awards and recognitions, Dr. Flanagan was a very humble man, always respected everyone and talked in a calm and reassuring voice, and always listened carefully, even to ideas that did not seem too innovative or brilliant. He had obtained his Ph.D. from the Massachusetts Institute of Technology (MIT), was a member of the National Academy of Science, the National Academy of Engineering and a Fellow of the largest engineering organization (IEEE).

I felt honored and excited to be working with such a great man. I started my new "real" job the following week. I learned more and more about video coding and video compression, and within a couple of months, I was able to publish my first research paper in low-bit-rate video coding in a well-respected conference proceeding. I enjoyed the work and made good progress, published more research papers and traveled to major research conferences and gave presentations. Dr. Flanagan was an outstanding mentor, coach, and researcher. He had an exceptionally sharp mind and always preferred simple ideas.

While I worked at that university, the Internet was expanding and every day new web-based applications would allow people to share ideas and communicate through this amazing online platform. In the early days of the Internet, a number of new online features allowed groups to promote new ideas and talk about current social, political and other issues. One of these new online forums was called "Newsgroups." Anyone could create a Newsgroup on a new topic and others could apply to become members of a specific Newsgroup. Since I was still very much interested in what was going on in Afghanistan, one day looking though the list of Newsgroups, I noticed that there was one dedicated to events in Afghanistan. The Newsgroup had been created by a student in one of the universities in the United States. Whenever I had free time, I would read articles about current events and the war in Afghanistan, and sometimes I would post articles there as well.

Since I lived about an hour and a half away from my work, in the evenings to avoid heavy traffic on the roads, I would leave the office later than everyone else and use some of my free time to read Newsgroup articles online. One day I saw an article from an Afghan student at Stanford University asking for anyone who could help him create a petition to help the Afghan children who were orphaned by the war. I was more than willing to help and worked with that Stanford student to create a petition to seek support from others. The petition was posted on that Afghan Newsgroup with our names and contact information.

Then one evening before going home I received an email from a young Afghan girl who was a student at one of the top and highly respected universities in the United States. Her name was Negah and in her short note she addressed me as "brother." She stated that she was also willing to help and support us with our petition and at the bottom of her email she mentioned that her family had relationships with a family who had the same last name as mine. I didn't think too much of it and quickly replied back to her, thanking her for her support and was curious to find out more about the family she mentioned. I asked her for additional information on their relationships with that family that had the same last name as ours.

To be honest, on my drive home, I started thinking more about this young girl, Negah. Who was she? She for sure was a smart and intelligent girl to have been admitted at one of the top universities in the United States. The next morning I arrived at the office and after turning on my computer, I saw another email from Negah; I quickly opened the email and noticed that this time she did not start the email with the word "brother" and also gave me more information about her family's relationships with the other family that had the same last name as ours. I now knew that the family she was talking about was related to my family. They were distant relatives of my father. I again sent her an email thanking her and telling her that we were related to the family she had mentioned and also started to ask some specific questions about her. In that email, I included some information about myself and what I was doing.

During the next few days and weeks, we started communicating via email, learning more about each other, our interests and views on almost every topic from politics to social issues. I was really fascinated by her level of maturity and how intelligent she was and truly enjoyed our email exchanges. I learned that she was a senior in college, the founder and president of the Afghan Student Association at her university, and that she was about eight years younger than me. Despite this age gap, we both enjoyed this "cyber" pen pal relationship.

Since this was the early days of the Internet and mobile phones and smartphones were not as widely available as consumer devices as they are today, we found another easier medium to correspond. Since I worked on large UNIX-based computers, I learned that there was a UNIX command that would allow two people connected on the same network to chat with each other in real-time. I taught that command to Negah, and soon we started chatting over the Internet. She would chat with me during her free time from the computer lab in the Engineering Department at her university. We were pioneers in exploring new frontiers of the Internet and its capabilities. My admiration and fascination started to grow for this young woman day by day, but I didn't even know how she looked like.

I finally decided I wanted to go and see her in person and she agreed to meet with me. Without telling anyone about the real purpose of my trip, I purchased a plane ticket and flew to where she lived. We had arranged for a place to meet close to her university and I arrived 10 or 15 minutes early and waited for her. She had given me a rough description of herself without too many details. I only knew that she was 21 years old, petite, and had curly short brown hair, and a few other minor details. I had also given her some clues about how I looked. I was getting a bit nervous and was sure she was even more nervous, sitting in this café where we were going to meet.

At the precise time of our meeting, I saw this beautiful petite young woman with brown curly hair enter. I knew by just looking at her that it was Negah.

I got up and smiled at her and without any hesitation she walked toward me, said "Hi," and we shook hands before she sat in front of me. She looked beautiful, wearing a nice blue dress and looking a bit nervous. So we slowly started to talk and laughed about how we ended up there. I asked her about her school and studies and she asked me about my years in France and my current research at the university. After about an hour or so we had become really comfortable with each other and talked about anything and everything. We stayed in that café for a few hours and then decided to go for a walk.

We walked for a while, again talking and laughing, and it seemed as if we had known each other for years. We ended up going to a restaurant for lunch and then she had to leave for an appointment she needed to keep, but she promised to see me again the next day before my flight back home.

Negah had immigrated to the United States when she was very young after spending about a year in Italy. She grew up in a fairly conservative Afghan family of seven siblings (four brothers and three sisters) and was commuting to her university for more than an hour and half each way every day of the week. Despite growing up between two cultures, she respected her family very much and did not want to disappoint them in any way. Although she was young, she seemed wise and held on to her pride of being an Afghan American. The next day my flight was scheduled for the evening. I had time during the day and was hoping to spend it with Negah. She arrived early at the place we were going to meet and we enjoyed a light breakfast together. We again talked and talked like old friends who had known each other forever.

We spent the entire day walking and talking and before leaving for the airport, I asked her if I could have a picture of her. By then, she had built enough trust in me to share one of her photos. She agreed and found one of her photos in her bag and gave it to me. I took that photo and put it in my wallet and said goodbye to her, leaving for the airport.

Back at home, I was sitting in front of my computer one day as my youngest sister, Mina, caught me reading an email from Negah and saw her picture. She went and told Mom and Grandma Bobo Jaan about it. I first told Mom about Negah then Grandma, Bobo Jaan showing them the photo Negah had given to me. They both saw that she was a beautiful, educated young lady and also realized that I wanted to spend the rest of my life with her. Negah and I kept our communication over the Internet, and I finally got the courage to tell her that I had fallen in love with her and wanted to spend the rest of my life with her. Without making it too obvious, she admitted that she felt the same way.

Following our traditions, I asked my Mom to fly to the West Coast and ask her parents for her hand in marriage and allow their daughter Negah to marry her son. My Mom and my sister Mina flew to California and after meeting with her family, the family asked to see me and talk to me. We made a second trip with my Mom and Baaba this time, and they finally agreed for me to marry their daughter. A few months later, Negah and I got engaged. We had a small engagement party with close relatives and friends in California. Our engagement lasted for about five months before we got married. I went to visit her whenever I could. I would send her postcards from everywhere I traveled for conferences and to this day she has kept them all, as well as all of our email exchanges.

Negah's family had immigrated to the United States in the early 80s, and she lived with her parents, brothers and sisters. Similar to my family, she grew up in a large family. Her family had moved to the United States, leaving everything behind in December of 1980, and like many other refugee families, they had to rebuild a new life for themselves. Negah's brothers were extremely hard working and within a short period of time, they were able to own their own business and lived a very comfortable life.

By December of 1992 we were married. After the wedding, she moved to the East Coast as I had just started a new job in a large telecommunications company. Six months after our wedding, Negah's dad passed away from cancer and I saw her going through a tough time. I would come home from work and her face looked as if she had cried all day, but she was pretending to hold her sorrows in.

Two years after our marriage, our son Eli was born in September of 1994, another very happy moment in our lives. All of my former struggles, my love of family, my passions, and my life had led me to the next phase of my life, and that was, and is, as a father. Eli, with his big brown eyes, was a handsome baby boy, very active from the day he was born. Negah and I were now responsible for this little boy, as he brought so much more joy and happiness into our lives. We soon realized that babies do not sleep through the nights because Eli would wake up every two hours. As inexperienced parents, we had many funny moments trying to feed him. He was a difficult and picky eater. We both enjoyed watching Eli grow up, learning new things to do, and something he really enjoyed doing was to watch the *"Barney"* show on TV non-stop for hours. He had memorized the Barney song, before talking or learning other words and when he was just over six months old, he would make sounds trying to sing the Barney song.

At about nine months old, he would sing, "I da da," meaning, "I love you," from Barney. We lived in a small town close to my work and almost every weekend we would spend time with the rest of the family about an hour away. Everyone adored Eli. The kids in the family would fight with each other over holding him. When he started to learn how to walk, he decided that walking was for lazy people; he would literally run. He loved chocolate chip cookies and orange juice and that was the only kind of food he would eat without being forced.

Around the time Eli was 11 months old, work for me changed, as the major telecommunications company I worked for split into three smaller companies. We ended up moving to Texas, where I started to work for a smaller regional telephone company. We did not know much about Texas. We just knew that the weather in Texas was much warmer than what we were used to on the East Coast; however, we did not have any idea about the length of the summer seasons in Texas and how hot it would get. We arrived in Texas in January of 1996 and rented a single-story small house there. Our move to Texas was handled by the company and we arrived there a couple of days before the movers arrived. That month of January of 1996, the weather was cold in Texas and we even had some light snow followed by a light ice storm. But we soon realized that the winter season in Texas would not last long.

Around the middle of April, the weather started to get warmer and in May the temperature reached 90 degrees or higher. The following months, June, July, August, September, and even a good part of October, the weather was hot. I have to admit that first summer in Texas was hard and long, something that we did not expect but slowly adjusted to.

Work was going well, the company was much smaller than my previous company, and I enjoyed working and interacting with all my coworkers. My boss John also came from the same major telecommunications company I had worked for and besides being a really sharp minded individual, he was a terrific human being. My new company started to buy other regional telephone companies and slowly got larger. It changed its name a few times through mergers and acquisitions and, in the end, purchased the major telecommunications company I had worked for on the East Coast. I felt I had made a full circle. My career in my company was advancing, as I was recognized with several major awards, and in 2008 I was awarded the prestigious Science and Technology Medal Award. I was also awarded more than 50 issued United States Patents for some key innovations in the area of Multimedia and Networking.

After a month or so, we decided to build a house in another part of town. This was the first time we were building a new house and it was an exciting time for both of us. During one of our visits to the construction site, we met our new neighbors, who were also building a new house. While inside our house, I heard a lady speaking French in the next house that was being built. All excited, I went outside to meet them. Her name was Virginia and she was from the Dijon region of France. With her American husband Tom, they had three daughters. The youngest daughter, Alice, was the same age as Eli and she was running around talking in mixed French and English. Within 6 months, our house was built and we moved in. Eli found a new best friend in Alice. They were inseparable. We loved her like our own child and she would spend countless hours playing with Eli in our house. They would ride in a little red jeep together or ride their bikes on our cul-de-sac.

When Eli was 3-years old, Negah got pregnant with our daughter, Noor. She was born in December of 1998 and brought even more joy into our lives. Noor was an angel from the day she was born in a private clinic in Texas. She was a quiet and happy baby, always smiling and playing by herself. When she was a few days old, Noor became severely ill. The doctor suspected that she might have meningitis. But fortunately she did not and after spending a couple of days in the hospital, she came home. Now that we had some experience with Eli, taking care of Noor was much easier and she was also an easier baby. Eli loved his newborn sister and smothered her with kisses all day long. He sometimes would get jealous of her getting too much attention, but overall he enjoyed playing with her.

Alice would be in our home most of the time and all three managed to get along fairly well, only occasionally fighting over the red jeep. Eli was extremely active and full of energy, running all day and not paying too much attention to eating or drinking. He had an obsession with dinosaurs and would buy a new plastic toy each time his Mom took him shopping. He played with Legos, cars, basketball, soccer, and tennis; and the only time he liked sitting still was for putting jigsaw puzzles together, an activity that other kids his age did not have much interest in. He would not leave the floor until his jigsaw puzzle was completed and would ask you to sit there with him and help at times to achieve his goal of finishing it. We were mesmerized at his concentration level at the age of two given how easily he became bored with most "quiet" activities.

Noor was the opposite. She enjoyed having her meals and played peacefully by herself for hours with her dolls, a purse over her shoulder, and a pair of binoculars sitting on the stairway with a cute backpack on her back. She also loved playing teacher and having "pretend" students or pretending she was a doctor or nurse and having a stethoscope around her neck and checking us.

Since Eli was such an active little boy, by the time he was almost four both Negah and I agreed that we needed to find an activity for him for expending his energy. As we both enjoyed sports, we enrolled him in gymnastics when he was three. Later, at the age of four, we enrolled him in soccer. Eli developed a passion for soccer from day one; he lived and breathed soccer from then on. The August prior to his fifth birthday, because he was born in September, public schools only accepted children 5-years old by September 1 and Eli was ready to go to school and not quite the age limit for public school, we decided to enroll him in a private school. It was a great Christian school. At the beginning, he was really excited to go to school, but after a couple of weeks he started to resist going. Therefore,

Negah started volunteering all day at his school and as Eli made friends he soon felt more comfortable. Negah would also take Noor with her during her volunteer time in his class and Eli's classmates loved to have Noor around. She sat at one of the desks in the classroom and colored and wanted to work like the big kids.

During this time Eli learned how to write beautifully in cursive and could read and spell really well in kindergarten. He also took piano lessons with a Russian lady who thought every kid would grow up to be a Mozart. She was hard on Eli, so he lost interest after a few months. Meanwhile, Negah and Noor went to school with Eli for two years. After two years, we transferred Eli into a public school. During those two years at the private school, Noor was going to school, sitting quietly in Eli's classroom, and she learned her ABCs, her colors, and could count up to 50. When Eli received his kindergarten certificate, Noor also received an honorary diploma at the age of only two!

Negah remained involved in our children's education and pursued a Master's degree in Healthcare Administration that she successfully completed while taking care of everything else. I always knew that she was not just satisfied with only having an undergraduate degree and with her love for medicine now she could get involved in hospital work and do what she aspired to achieve. Noor was becoming even more adorable, and whenever I came home from work, she was waiting for me and would run into my arms, kiss my face, and hold on to me. She was my little princess and I enjoyed watching her learn new things every day.

I still remember the days she would sit on the stairs of our house with binoculars hanging around her neck, carrying her doll with a pair of cool shades and playing by herself. Eli was also excelling in school and had become a great soccer player in his age group. We enrolled him in a soccer club at the age of four. While some kids didn't know which goal to run towards or would get distracted in the middle of the field, Eli would make almost all of the goals for his team. He always made the top teams but also became a top player for the club. He had a keen eye for perfect passes and taking perfect corner shots for his team. He started to travel with his club for soccer competitions within the state of Texas and later on outside the Texas in the Olympic Development Program (ODP). We traveled to every single game and tournament he participated in and enjoyed watching him, rain or shine, cold or hot, every moment he was on the soccer field. Eli became known for his keen ball handling skills, his eye for headers, and for his hat tricks (straight three goals in a row). In middle school, Eli joined the school band under a fine director and played the oboe for two years. Unfortunately, soccer commitments got in the way and he dropped band in 8th grade, which was a tough decision for him, as he played this instrument beautifully.

I have several unforgettable memories of his outstanding soccer accomplishments. One particular memory that is engraved in my brain is when we were in Houston, playing for the State Championship. He was about 13 or 14 years old. We had won most of our games and qualified to play in the final game against a team from El Paso. The El Paso team was the favorite team to win that State Championship as they dominated the game from the beginning.

But a couple of minutes before half time, Eli scored a beautiful goal from about 30 yards from the opposing goal, and our team was ahead 1-0. During the second half of the game, the El Paso team continued their domination; however, our defense did not allow them to score.

When the game was about to end, something happened close to the goal we defended. The referee decided to give a red card to our goal keeper, expelling him from the game and allowing a penalty kick to the El Paso team. We were all shocked. I saw Eli taking our goalkeeper's gloves before he left the field and he stood in the goal, making himself the de facto goalkeeper. One of the strong players from the El Paso team placed the ball in the penalty spot and the referee blew the whistle, signaling to the El Paso team player to go ahead and take the penalty kick. All the parents on our side were waiting anxiously to see what would happen. I then looked over my shoulder and saw Negah reciting a prayer quietly with tears coming down her face. The El Paso team player kicked the ball as hard as he could and out of nowhere Eli jumped to the side of the goal where the ball was about to enter the goal and stopped the penalty kick. We all screamed with joy and all of his teammates were on top of him. A couple of minutes later, the game ended and Eli's team had won the State Championship.

Not many kids can brag to have gotten to State Championship games a few times. Eli's English soccer coach that day hugged him and told him that there are not many soccer players who could brag about scoring a goal and saving a penalty kick in the same championship game. Eli continued to make even more progress in soccer and by the time he was in high school, he was selected to play for the United States Soccer Development Academy team. Several Division 1 soccer colleges and highly respected universities were interested in recruiting him, as he was doing very well academically and athletically. During his senior year in high school, he de-committed from college soccer and decided to focus more on his academics and play soccer for fun.

He and his team won the intramural championships for soccer last year at his university, and Negah and I even went to watch him play during his intramural games just like the old times. Today Eli is in his last year of college, majoring in Neuroscience and completing certificates in both Business and Computer Science. We are extremely proud of him. He has also made good choices in friends, whom we also adore as part of our family. He has given us a lot to be proud of and we will always cherish our days of traveling with him to his practice and games.

When Noor was a toddler, she joined ballet, then gymnastics. Later she would follow Eli in everything he did. She also went to the same private Christian school for pre-K and Kindergarten and started to play soccer. She joined Kumon, just like her big brother, and wanted to play the piano, which she did until 8th grade and took some voice lessons for that summer of 8th grade. During her last piano recital, she sang and performed, "My Heart Will Go On." She also excelled in soccer like her big brother and took guitar lessons for a few months. She was well coordinated (she was the only two-year-old riding a scooter in the neighborhood), fast, and always scoring goals. She played up in the age 10 group's top soccer team when she was only 9-years old. She played soccer for a few years and then decided to switch to volleyball for middle school.

Volleyball became her passion. She was not a tall player at 5'6" but she was extremely well coordinated, quick in defense and great at passing the ball. We enrolled her in one of the biggest volleyball clubs in Austin. In her first season of club volleyball, she was the only player in the history of the club who served 25 times in a row in one of the competitions and won the set. Her poster-sized photo was framed on the wall of the club and is hanging today in our home office. Noor continued to excel in school and in volleyball. We enjoyed watching her on the volleyball courts, traveling with her all over the United States to participate in competitions. She had become our superstar and hardworking girl; she excelled in school and thrived both academically and athletically.

Negah and I were extremely proud of both Eli and Noor, as they had given us so much joy and happiness. We moved before Noor's freshman year, as Negah got a job with one of the well-respected school districts in town and Noor attended the high school where it had won previous football and volleyball state championships. Since the school was not aware of Noor's talent during her freshman year, she was placed on the junior varsity team at her high school and she soon was respected for her volleyball and academic success as well as her sweet personality.

During club games, she had Ivy League coaches and other top Division 1 volleyball coaches observing and highly interested in her. During her sophomore year in high school, Noor became the Libero for the varsity team and caught the eyes of every coach in and out of town, as well as college coaches around the country with club volleyball. Noor loved her varsity coach dearly as she pushed her hard and recognized her talent, and she loved Noor as well. She also had respect for her club coach who trusted Noor on the court to be the glue of the team. He was thrilled to see big name college coaches be on the sidelines during their big tournaments watching Noor and our team.

Noor finished her high school season during her sophomore season as No. 7 Libero in the country. She received many accolades that year, such as Defensive MVP, first team All-District as the only other sophomore from the District and Academic All District and was chosen by the local newspaper as the Newcomer of the Year. Her photo appeared in local newspaper for her hard work and dedication. During her club season in January of her sophomore year, we traveled to San Antonio, Texas, for a large volleyball tournament. She started that tournament really strong, not only defending, but also scoring points with outstanding jump serves. In one of the plays, she lost her balance and landed in an unstable manner and injured one of her knees.

Noor was a tough girl and rarely cried, but after that fall she screamed and started crying. I knew that she was hurt badly. When we got back home, we took her to one of the best orthopedic surgeons in town and after an MRI he diagnosed her with a complete tear of one of her knee's ACL ligaments. She needed surgery in the middle of the school year. I knew she would recover from this injury and surgery and would come back even stronger. She went through a major reconstructive knee surgery, worked really hard to come back and recover. The local newspaper published an article about Noor's return and how hard she had worked, but unfortunately she had not given her ACL more than six 6 months to heal so she had a partial ACL tear on the same knee. She worked tirelessly to recover for the second time and came back even stronger for the playoff games at the end of the season. Her teammates and parents were thrilled to have her contributions.

Despite her injury and recovery, many great academic Division 1 schools, including Ivy League universities, still wanted her to become part of their volleyball program, but instead she decided to focus more on her academics and completed high school and graduated early at the end of her junior year. She was admitted at the University of Texas, Austin and is looking forward to becoming a nurse someday to help others. I know that the kids' achievements were due to their own talent and hard work, but Negah also played an important role in their success. Knowing the kids' capabilities, she held them to high standards for everything they did and dedicated her life to their achievements and success. She scarified her own yearning of wanting a career for many years to see that the kids grow up to be good and kind human beings with good values. We are extremely blessed and proud of both kids and are looking forward to the next chapters of their lives as Eli is graduating from college this year.

11 FINDING MY CHILDHOOD FRIEND: NADJIB

About 10 years ago, while traveling to a family function in another state, I was talking with someone I didn't know very well. During the conversation he told me that he had family in Europe and had just returned from a visit. I asked him about the Afghan community where his family resided in Europe, and how they were doing. He told me that they were doing well. He also shared that he had met there a new Afghan refugee family, and the man he talked with had attended the same French high school I graduated from. I asked the man's name.

Nadjib was the name.

When I heard that name my curiosity peaked and shot up intensely. I kept asking for more details on what he looked like, his age and what region of Afghanistan he came from. I wanted to learn if this Nadjib could possibly be the same Nadjib who had been my best friend in school. The information this man provided gave me renewed hope that I may have finally found one of my childhood best friends.

I asked the man at that family function if he could find me a phone number for the person named Nadjib who lived in the same area in Europe as his family did. Since I didn't know him really well, he promised me that the next time he talked to his family in Europe, he would ask them to find Nadjib's phone number and he would pass it to one of my relatives that he knew.

A couple of months later, in the lobby of a hotel during a business trip, I received a phone call from one of my relatives, who gave me a phone number for a person named Nadjib who lived in Europe. I immediately realized where this phone number had come from and thanked him for giving it to me. I wrote the number on a piece of paper and then thought about what to do next. Of course, I couldn't be certain that the phone number I had in my hand actually belonged to my best friend Nadjib, whom I hadn't seen in decades. And even if this was his phone number, would he recognize me? Would he still be the same short and funny best friend I knew so long ago? After more hesitation, I realized that because of the time zone difference, it was after 11:00 p.m. where he lived, but I could no longer wait and decided to call the number.

The phone started ringing and after a few rings, a lady picked up and said hello in Dari. After saying hello back to her, I asked if I could talk to Nadjib, and she said yes.

I next heard a fairly strong voice saying "Hi" and quickly asking me who I was to call so late and was everything okay. I apologized and said I may be one of your old friends and wanted to talk to you. He asked for my name, but I first wanted to give him some clues about our childhood and see if he would recognize me:

"Do you remember Yasseen?"

"Do you remember 2nd grade and a teacher named Ismael Khan?"

Without me saying another word, he called me by name and asked:

"Are you him?"

Suddenly we were both filled with emotions. He then asked me to wait for a minute, as he needed to go to another room in his apartment. I waited impatiently; then I heard his voice again on the other end of the line. He asked me where I was and how I was doing. He said he had often thought about me and Yasseen and wasn't sure if we were still alive.

After giving him an update about myself and telling him that I was doing fine, I asked him how he was doing and if he had news from Yasseen. He started to talk about Yasseen first. Yasseen had to quit school to support his father and his family and after the war had started, his family moved back to the province of Panjshir, where they were from. He said that the last time he saw Yasseen was on the streets of Kabul, telling Nadjib that they were getting ready to leave Kabul as the city was becoming unsafe for them. He was not sure where Yasseen was or even if he had survived decades of war and conflicts. Like me, he said he hoped that someday he would be able to find and see Yasseen again.

He then told me that he was worried about talking too much, as he had so much to talk about and also told me that he had difficulty sleeping at night and did not want me to end up with a costly phone bill. I quickly put him at ease and told him that the least I could do was to pay for a phone call talking to my best friend that I had missed so dearly, after so many years. Then he started talking.

He told me that when we were in our senior year of high school, one of the members of the school's communist association had spied on him, which resulted in Nadjib being arrested by Afghan Secret Service agents. Nadjib had lived in the old part of the city, in an old house with his father, his mother, and his siblings. I believe it was still too difficult for him to talk about being arrested by the Afghan Secret Service Agents in front of his family.

Those agents did not show a shred of humanity or decency. I could still sense the pain of what must have gone on at the headquarters of the Afghan Secret Service (Khadamat-e Aetela'at-e Dawlati, KHAD). I have heard horror stories from other friends who were arrested and tortured there. The Soviet interrogators had trained their Afghan counterparts really well in all forms of torture, including pulling out finger and toe nails, severe beatings, keeping prisoners awake for multiple days, not providing food to political prisoners for extended periods of time, using electricity to shock political inmates, etc. One of my close friends who was arrested and spent several weeks at the KHAD torture factory told me that he became so tired of being badly beaten every time they interrogated him that at one point he begged one of the agents that he would admit to anything they wished and would sign any confession documents that they wanted him to sign because he was ready to die and be done with his misery. But the agents kept telling him that they wanted the real truth from his own mouth.

Political prisoners were not allowed to have a lawyer to defend them. A "revolutionary court" made of ignorant and inhumane communist party members would charge innocent prisoners with phony crimes against the state and hand out harsh punishments, including frequent death sentences. Another friend told me that prisoners were tried in large groups and after the so called "revolutionary court prosecutor" had read phony made-up charges against the innocent poor Afghans who were their captives, each prisoner was given five minutes to present his defense. Almost all the time, the inmates were found guilty by the "revolutionary court."

In one instance a friend told me that while he was waiting for his turn to go through the "tribunal," two young Afghan men in their early 20s were sentenced to death. After handing them the harsh sentence, the "revolutionary tribunal" judge asked them if they had anything to say in their defense. My friend, who was really scared and waiting with the rest of the people for their turns, said that what happened next was something you only see in movies. The two young Afghan men who were facing the revolutionary court started to talk one after another. The first young man told the court that he was honored to be found guilty and sentenced to death by people who were slaves of the Soviets and worked for a puppet government. He continued:

"Life is only worth living when a man is free . . . I am not afraid of dying in the hands of corrupt people like the so called "revolutionary court," members who are without any honor or dignity."

His young friend who was also sentenced to death repeated something similar. They were both taken away soon after.

Sometimes these savage agents of the KHAD actually used the prisoners' own loved ones as an instrument of torture too. Another good friend of mine, who had been a prisoner at KHAD, told me that in one of the most painful events he had ever witnessed he saw a young man who must have been 18 or 19 years old being interrogated after a severe beating session that left him bloodied and bruised in the same interrogation room as my friend. He saw the brutal agents carrying that young man's father into the same interrogation room. His Baaba was in really bad shape, beaten and bloodied, tortured and really weak. The young man, seeing his father in that shape, started crying and wanted to hug him, but the agents prevented him from getting close to his father.

I fully understood why Nadjib could not talk about his time in KHAD or prison in Kabul. While talking, Nadjib kept worrying about my phone bill and I kept telling him not to worry, that I would pay the bill; that I was there to listen to him. I felt he needed his story told and shared with someone who cared about him, and I certainly cared about my old best friend. After his release from prison, Nadjib took his family and escaped Afghanistan where they became refugees in Pakistan.

Realizing what the Afghan communist regime and the Soviet invaders were doing in Afghanistan, Nadjib had decided to join one of the

Afghan resistance movements and fight the communists and the Soviet invaders. Since he was a smart, young and brave man, working with the Afghan resistance movement, he was assigned more responsibilities and was soon put in charge of a large group of Afghan fighters. He then talked about war and how it changed him forever. He had made many good friends while fighting the Soviets and also lost many good friends. He himself was injured several times. He told me that his physical scars from years of fighting are not that painful anymore, but what was still keeping him awake at nights were the emotional scars of losing friends, seeing poor Afghan families and innocent civilians, including women and children, being decimated by indiscriminate killings, bombings and land mines.

Since he had become a good commander, winning several battles against the Soviets, Nadjib was given a war name and an honorary title and was highly respected amongst the Mujahedin. Somehow, during this time, he had managed to get married and now had five children who were all with him in Europe. He told me that after the defeat of the Soviet Union and the start of the Afghan civil war, he became really depressed and disillusioned seeing all these brave Afghans who were once united in fighting the invaders, then fighting each other for power. He said he knew that his job was done, as he was no longer interested in the next fight.

We spoke on the phone for more than two hours, and since it was late for him, I told him that I would call him again soon and hopefully would see him someday soon. After we said our goodbyes, I left the hotel lobby to go for a walk. While walking, still very emotional, I thought about my friend and what he had just told me, the hardships he had endured, and remembered this quote I used to hear from Grandpa Baaba Jaan:

"Man is harder than rock and softer than water."

For sure, my friend Nadjib was harder than rock. I am still hoping to see him someday, talk for hours, and share stories of our lives.

12 THE DEFEAT OF THE SOVIET UNION – THE TALIBANIZATION OF AFGHANISTAN

As you now know I was badly injured during the Afghan communists' military coup backed by the Soviet Union. Over the years I've wondered why these events happened and why some individuals in power become so cruel that they kill innocent people who do not agree with them. I strongly believe that power can change people, because I have personally observed it during the time when the communists in Afghanistan became powerful. Whenever I hear about cruelties and brutalities around the world, I often remember this beautiful quote:

"Nearly all men can stand adversity, but if you want to test a man's character, give him power."

I have always wondered why the Soviet Union decided to invade Afghanistan. It was not a country full of natural resources or a country with direct access to the Indian Ocean. I soon came to the realization that Afghanistan's location made it a clear target for superpowers to try to either have direct or indirect influence or dominance over it. Looking at the history of Afghanistan, major conquerors from the Mongols to Alexander the Great to the British Empire to the Soviets have tried to conquer and dominate Afghanistan.

But no one has succeeded.

There are two main reasons for this: one is related to the terrain, as Afghanistan is a very mountainous and rugged country, and the second reason is its people. The people of Afghanistan are free spirited, fiercely independent, extremely proud and brave people. They are at the same time one of the most hospitable people in the world, welcoming and very friendly. I may be biased, but I believe that Afghanistan is also one of the most beautiful countries in the world.

Going back to the question of why the Soviet Union wanted to invade Afghanistan, it is now clear that during the Cold War, the United States established extremely friendly relationships with Pakistan and, prior to the Iranian Revolution, with Iran and its regime under the rule of the Shah, Iran worked closely with the United States. Afghanistan was sandwiched between countries that were clearly very friendly with the United States. When President Daoud Khan of Afghanistan decided to become closer to the West and attempted to distance himself from the Soviet Union, it became highly alarming and dangerous for the Soviet leaders to accept losing Afghanistan in this chess game to the United States and, therefore, they had to take action.

In December of 1979, the Soviet Union invaded Afghanistan militarily to support the Afghan communist regime that was battling the Afghan Freedom Fighters, commonly referred to as the Mujahedin. The Soviet occupation of Afghanistan lasted more than nine years and, according to historians, killing between 850,000 to 2 million Afghan civilians. Millions of other Afghans fled the country as refugees, mostly to neighboring countries such as Pakistan and Iran, where they mostly lived under refugee tents in dire conditions. A small percentage of the educated

Afghan refugees with means and connections to the West, immigrated to Western European countries, Australia and the United States.

The Afghan resistance movement against the Afghan communist regime was started by Afghans fighting a puppet government that was installed by the Soviets. Initially the Mujahedin fought the oppressive communist regime with very little support from the outside and with simple and rudimentary weapons. When the Soviets invaded Afghanistan, the West and especially the United States, fearing the expansion of Soviet dominance in the region, decided to intervene and help the Afghan resistance movement. From the beginning of the Afghan war with the Soviets, the United States tried to unify the Afghan resistance movement by telling the Afghans that the communists did not believe in God and were against the majority of Muslim Afghans and their religion.

Afghanistan is an old and multiethnic society and the people of the country are made of a wide variety of ethno-linguistic groups. For the most part, all of these different ethnic groups lived with one another peacefully. Some of the key ethnic groups in Afghanistan are Pashtuns, Tajiks, Hazaras, Uzbeks, Turkmen, Nuristanis, and a few other minority groups. They all have their own languages, specific foods, traditions and cultural differences. (The two official languages in Afghanistan are Dari and Pashtu).

The conversion of Afghanistan into an Islamic society was started in the middle of the 7th century by the Arab Muslims. Afghanistan had become a Muslim country by the middle of the 10th century. But one region of Afghanistan called *"Kafiristan"* (land of the infidels) refused to convert to Islam until one of the Emirs by the name of Emir Abdul Rahman Khan forcefully converted them to Islam in the 1890s and renamed the region *"Nuristan"* (Land of Light). Most people living in the Nuristan region of Afghanistan are from the time when Alexander the Great established his settlement there. As one can see, Afghanistan is not a very uniform country in many different ways, but Islam has been the glue that somehow unified the country.

The United States became involved in the Afghan conflict after the Soviet Union's invasion of Afghanistan, providing financial and military support to the Afghan Mujahedin. During the Afghan war with the Soviets, a large number of foreign fighters came to help the Afghans fight the Soviet invaders, and most of them were from the Arab Muslim countries. This is also when Osama Bin Laden with a large group of his supported came to Afghanistan through Pakistan, to support the Afghan war against the Soviets. During that time, the United States supported unequivocally all the forces that fought the Soviet Union, including Osama Bin Laden. It is important to note that at one point the United States also supported Saddam Hussein during the Iran-Iraq war – *"the enemy of my enemy is my friend."*

In early 1989, the Soviet Union was defeated and decided to withdraw its troops from Afghanistan. The Soviets committed some of the worst atrocities against the Afghan people. Some scholars and observers believed that the Soviet Union committed genocide by killing hundreds of thousands of innocent Afghans to suppress their resistance. After the withdrawal of the Soviet troops from Afghanistan, the very weak and incompetent communist Afghan regime tried different policies to bring some type of stability and normalcy to Afghanistan.

At that time, the president of Afghanistan was Dr. Najibullah, who during the invasion by the Soviet Union was the head of the Afghan Secret Service when hundreds of thousands of innocent Afghans were arrested, tortured and killed. Dr. Najibullah was trying to play the role of a peacemaker after massacring large numbers of innocent people. It was just a matter of time before the communist regime would collapse, as the

Mujahedin forces were approaching the capital city of Kabul. Finally the Mujahedin forces took control of the government in Kabul, and Dr. Najibullah escaped and sought refuge at the United Nations buildings in Kabul.

What really happened next is a tragedy that not only impacted Afghanistan, but the entire world. After the defeat of the Soviet Union in Afghanistan, the United States no longer showed any interest in being actively involved in Afghanistan. They had achieved their goal of defeating their arch enemy, the Soviet Union, having handed the Soviets their own "Vietnam"; but the plight of Afghanistan and its people were no longer of significant interest to the United States.

A few years ago I watched a fascinating movie, "Charlie Wilson's War," based on a true story. The movie portrayed a United States Congressman (Charlie Wilson) who played an instrumental role in defeating the Soviet Union in Afghanistan. After the Soviets were defeated, Congressman Wilson went back to Washington asking the United States government officials, other powerful Congressmen and Senators to help stabilize Afghanistan by building schools, roads, hospitals and help with the creation of a stable government.

But most of these powerful politicians, some graduates of well-known Ivy League universities, did not foresee what was about to happen next that not only impacted the poor Afghans and that region but the entire world, including the United States. I remember clearly what Charlie Wilson said at the end of that movie:

"We defeated the Soviet Union in Afghanistan and by abandoning Afghanistan at the end we fucked up." He was one of the few politicians who was worried that an unstable Afghanistan could endanger the rest of the world, and unfortunately that is exactly what was about to happen next.

After the Soviets left Afghanistan, a civil war broke out between the different factions who had been fighting the invaders. Regional powers, especially Iran and Pakistan, encouraged by the lack of interest from the West and the United States, started to support specific groups, providing them with military and financial support. This power vacuum also encouraged powerful and rich people like Osama Bin Laden to exploit the situation to their advantage and see if they could establish a base of operations for their new endeavors. The civil war continued, killing more innocent Afghan. During the Democratic Administration of President Bill Clinton in the United States, General Parvez Musharraf, who had become the president of Pakistan through a military coup, was encouraged by the United States to create a military force and somehow try to end the civil war in Afghanistan.

That is how the Taliban movement was born.

The word Talib is an Arabic word meaning "seeker of knowledge" or "student." That word is not a native word in either Dari or Pashtu languages of Afghanistan. The word Taliban is a pseudo-Pashtu name created by the Pakistani government. The core of the Taliban movement was created in Pakistan with a mix of Pakistani and Afghan fundamentalists, trained by the Pakistani Inter-Service Intelligence (ISI). With the financial, logistical and military support of Pakistan, the Taliban entered Afghanistan from the south, quickly capturing towns and villages and finally reaching Kandahar, where they created their base.

With the continued support of Pakistan, the Taliban movement recruited young Afghan refugees and other desperate young men to fight with them and quickly took over most of Afghanistan. The Taliban's rule in Afghanistan was marked by inhumane brutalities and a complete disregard for basic human rights, especially of women's rights. Girls were not allowed to go to school anymore, and eventually the Taliban decided to close all girls' schools.

They ruled by fear, forcing men to grow beards and creating a new police unit or "moral force" to ensure that their rules were followed by every man, woman and child. If anyone did not follow their strict guidance, severe public punishments were administered. They started cutting off the hands of thieves in public and turned the main football (soccer) stadium in Kabul into their main public execution arena for people who were accused of committing murder, adultery, and other crimes that they believed justified execution.

The Taliban also did significant damage to our homeland by destroying thousands of old, valuable treasures, and historical sites that they viewed as un-Islamic symbols. Not knowing or maybe not caring that this beautiful old country was not always a Muslim country throughout its history, the Taliban took no interest in Afghanistan's unique and precious history or its artifacts going back thousands of years.

One sad and flagrant example of the Taliban's ignorance of and their violent approach to everything was the destruction of the majestic Buddhas of Bamiyan. The Buddhas of Bamiyan were statues from the 4th and 5th centuries. They were monumental statues of standing Buddhas carved into the side of a cliff in the Bamyan region of Afghanistan where the Hazaras tribe of Afghanistan lived and still lives to this day.

The history and clear origin of the Hazaras have, unfortunately, not been fully explored and exposed. They have significant Asian descent with strong ties to Turks and Mongols, as their physical attributes, facial bone structures and parts of their culture and language resemble those of Mongolians and Central Asian Turks. There is also a strong belief that Hazaras have direct Mongolian roots.

The Buddhas consisted of two statues, a smaller and a larger one, and represented the classic blended style of the arts during the 4th and 5th centuries in that part of the world. They were 35 and 53 meters tall, standing beautifully overlooking the amazing valley of Bamyan.

The Taliban decided to dynamite and destroy this valuable historical treasure and landmark in March of 2001 by orders from their leader Mullah Mohammed Omar. Their Afghan Minister of Foreign Affairs claimed that the destruction was about carrying out Islamic religious iconoclasm. International opinion strongly condemned the destruction of the Buddhas, which in the following years was primarily viewed as an example of the extreme religious intolerance of the Taliban. Japan and Switzerland, among others, have pledged support for the rebuilding of the statues.

Ironically this climate of fear brought some form of stability into regions under the Taliban control, as people no longer suffered from the killings caused by the civil war. But people still lived under another form of terror. None of the Taliban rules and guidelines were in line with the proper teachings of Islam. With their ignorance they wrongly believed that everything they were doing was sanctioned by the religion they believed in.

General Pervez Musharraf, by creating the Taliban movement and actively supporting them financially and militarily, lacked a complete understanding of how he would bear responsibility for not only endangering Afghanistan, but also for endangering Pakistan, his own country, and the entire world. In 2014, after falling from grace, General Musharraf was booked and charged with treason for some other activities he was engaged in against his nation in 2007. Today the Taliban are still powerful, not only in Afghanistan, but also where they were created, in Pakistan.

The only group resisting the Taliban was led by a Tajik commander known as Ahmad Shah Massoud, who was forced to a small region in the northern part of Afghanistan. By then Osama Bin Laden and his army of foreign fighters were all in Afghanistan. They had established very close ties with the Taliban, financing some of their operations. Unfortunately most of the Taliban leadership was made up of uneducated clerics, allowing Osama bin Laden to become the de facto ruler of Afghanistan. Osama Bin Laden had a bigger agenda -- emboldened by the defeat of the Soviet Union, his next objective was to start fighting the United States. The only way he could fight the United States was through terrorist activities and, therefore, he created a number of terrorist training camps in Afghanistan. He planned and financed the terrorist activities of September 11, killing more than 3000 innocent people.

* * * *

I often hear from some really well-educated conservative and liberal American politicians that these Muslim extremists committing acts of terror against the West are doing them because of our Western values and our way of life. It is ironic to me to hear statements like this. To most of these extremist terrorists, the core of their arguments with the United States and the West is based on what they claim to be the one-sided foreign policies in the Middle East. They may not adhere to some of the values and ways of life in the West, but it is naive to believe and promote that this is their main reason to fight the United States.

There is no justification for terrorism and killing innocent people for any reason. I don't know what God and what religion would condone the killing of innocent people in their names and open the gates of heaven to killers and terrorists.

As a Muslim, I was always taught that in Islam killing one innocent person is the same as killing all of humanity. I think it is the duty of all

Muslims and especially Muslim leaders to reject those who commit acts of terrorism in the name of Islam and be more proactive in propagating the message of peace and brotherhood.

Going back to Afghanistan and the reign of the Taliban, it is now clear that they allowed Osama Bin Laden to create and recruit for his terrorist activities in Afghanistan. This again shows the short-sightedness of the American foreign policy in supporting a dictator such as General Musharraf to create, finance, and support a movement like the Taliban that enabled Osama Ben Laden to terrorize the world. Compared to the cost of helping Afghanistan after the Soviets' defeat, by building schools, hospitals, roads and bridges (what some people call nation building) and establishing some type of stable government, compared to the cost of what happened in the following years (Tragedy of 9/11, wars in Afghanistan and Iraq, destabilization of the Middle East, emergence of other extremist groups such as ISIS, etc.) one can conclude that there was a missed opportunity to avoid the tragedies and wars that are still continuing.

After the horrific tragedies of September 11, and the justified involvement of the United States in Afghanistan to crush the Taliban and eliminate the Al Qaeda movement, the focus should have stayed there. Unfortunately, neoconservatives, in positions of power in the United States government, with their slanted idealism and unrealistic expectations, convinced the American government to invade Iraq and created a bigger mess that is now hard to manage and control.

I still believe that if superpowers such as the United States get involved in regional conflicts, they need to have long term plans that are well thought through. I remember General Colin Powell, before the war in Iraq, telling the camp that was pushing for the invasion of Iraq, a very insightful and powerful quote:

"If you break it you own it."

I sometimes wish that the United States had not abandoned Afghanistan after the Soviets' defeat.

I am certain that one day historians will analyze what happened during the 1980s in Afghanistan, and my only hope is that the next generation of powerful politicians learns from the huge missed opportunities and mistakes of the past and do not repeat the same mistakes again.

13 FINAL THOUGHTS

For the past several years, I kept telling Negah, Eli and Noor that someday I would write about my life and my past. As I mentioned at the beginning of this book, for someone like me, who is not an author, and did not learn English at an early age, writing a memoir or a short book has not been an easy task. I have to admit that my timing for starting to write this memoir is a bit ironic. In the past twelve months, I have been traveling for business more than usual, mainly from Texas to California. Since most modern airplanes these days have Wi-Fi onboard, I have typically use my time during these flights to work, check e-mails and perform other administrative tasks related to my job.

On one of the trips last year, once the flight took off, the flight attendant announced that the Wi-Fi system on that particular airplane was not functioning. I had more than three hours of flight time left and wanted to do something useful with my time. After a few minutes, I pulled out my laptop and decided to draft an outline for my memoir. As I was formulating the outline, I realized how lucky I have been, despite going through some difficult times in my life. That draft outline showed me that I was lucky enough to get a great education, immigrate to one of the best countries in the world, find Negah, have two wonderful children, secure a great job, and enjoy a loving extended family and many great friends.

It is not a great life experience to be badly injured in the prime years of one's life, but I often wonder what would have happened to me if I had not been injured. Would I have worked that hard to be awarded a scholarship to go to France? Would I have earned a Doctorate degree? Would I have had the opportunities I was given throughout my life?

When I read the first draft of my book, I noticed that there are events in our lives for which we may be able to control the outcome; but there are many other events that we cannot control when all we can do is deal with the consequences of those events and how we react after the fact. For example, I could not have controlled the rocket attack that injured me, but how I lived my life after that attack was under my control. Dealing with disappointments and failures is never easy, but now that I am in my early 50s, I do know that we don't always succeed in everything that we do in life.

The key lesson I learned is to never give up in the face of adversity. Always try to work hard and do the best you can; even if you fail you will always learn something. I know it is easy for me to say that we should always do our best and work hard; but what I have heard from many great thinkers and also learned in my own life is that hard work always beats talent. Admittedly, a combination of talent and hard work can significantly contribute to a successful life, but talent by itself will never guarantee successful outcomes in life.

Today, I still have scars from my injuries in my teenage years from the rocket attack, but they are just a reminder for me about how far I have come in life from its lowest points. Sometimes during the low moments, I did not see a reason to be alive; but I firmly believe that somehow my faith and the love of my family and friends kept hope alive for me. Looking back at the rich life I have lived so far, I consider myself one of the luckiest man on the face of this earth.

I will always remember that first year in France, dealing with so much hardship, being away from my loved ones, alone in a foreign country I knew very little about, my father a political prisoner back home, and the extremely difficult and challenging academic curriculum I had to succeed in. I will have to be honest and admit there were times I just wanted to give up, but in those dark moments, I remembered the hardships my parents went through so I could escape persecution, an uncertain future, go to Europe, get a good education and become a successful person for whom they would be proud of. Everything I have been able to do to become who I am today, is because of the love and support I received from so many people.

The love of my parents, siblings, grandparents, Aunts and uncles helped me to cope with very difficult dark days during the year I was injured. I am forever grateful to Uncle Abdul and his wife for helping me with my medical treatment; there is nothing I can do to repay them. The help and support of my first instructor in France, Mademoiselle Chaumet, provided me with a solid foundation, helping me to believe in myself and work harder. Her inspiration and support allowed me to successfully receive a great education. Meeting Professor Jim Flanagan and working with him is one of the honors that I will never forget. He not only had a very bright and intelligent engineering mind, but he also exemplified greatness, humility, and tolerance, and he valued human diversity as a great asset. He taught me the value of simple ideas and how they can change the world in the way he did that with his outstanding work in speech processing.

I am finally grateful to be a father and have Negah's love and support by my side. Eli and Noor have given us so much happiness and joy. You two are the bright stars of our lives and we are blessed and lucky to have you. You are both smarter than I am, and always remember that with hard work and dedication, anything is possible in life. I see so much potential in you and I am confident that you both will live rich and fulfilling lives and will pass on the same values and compassion to your own children someday.

Unfortunately not everyone in my homeland had the same opportunities I had. During the past three decades, Afghanistan has suffered too much misery. A generation of young Afghans experienced nothing but war and devastation. Millions of poor Afghan refugees have grown up in refugee camps, under tents in Pakistan or Iran, without adequate nutrition, healthcare or education. I don't know what happened to all the young children and babies who were born in those refugee camps.

Where are they today?

How many are still alive?

And what are they doing?

I am certain if they had the same luck that I had, today some of those young children could have been even more successful than me.

In the middle of this darkness, there are some amazing acts of humanity that give us all hope. There were many selfless individuals who sacrificed their lives to help the poor and the destitute. One example that comes to mind is the heroic acts of an Afghan medical doctor. When we lived in Kabul, across from our house lived a rich and powerful Afghan family living in a large and luxurious compound that occupied a few blocks. The father had a prominent and powerful position during King Zaher Shah's rule of Afghanistan. One of the sons studied at the University of Kabul Medical School and became a physician. His name was Dr. Abdullah Osman. He was a tall, handsome and rich young man, driving a nice Mercedes car, practicing medicine in Kabul. He lived with his wife and young children in one of the homes inside that compound.

His life changed one early morning when the communist Secret Service Agents came and arrested him for not actively supporting the communist government. He was taken to the infamous Secret Service headquarters (KHAD) and beaten, tortured and abused for months before they transferred him to another inferno, the "Pule Charkhi Prison." After spending a few years in that prison, they released him from prison as an apparently broken and changed man. Soon after his release he decided to escape Afghanistan and took his family to Pakistan. From Pakistan, he moved his family to the United States and decided that he himself would stay behind in Pakistan and help the Afghan refugees. He had no associations with any political factions and early on did not receive financial support from any organizations or governments. He decided to move closer to the Afghan refugee camps and provide whatever medical care he could provide. He did not do this humanitarian work for a just a few months; he dedicated the rest of his life to serving the poor and the destitute people of Afghanistan.

He could have come to the United States and become a successful physician. But during the time he spent in prison, he saw so many poor Afghan people in jail that no one cared about. He decided to make a difference. They had not broken him or his spirit.

Today he is back in Afghanistan, helping the large number of Afghan children who were orphaned by the decades of war. He is the Director of Operations for the International Orphan Care (http://www.orphanproject.org) in Kabul. He is someone who truly sacrificed everything to help others, and people like him are giving hope to humanity. Recently I watched a beautiful documentary by one of his daughters made about him. It is called "Postcards from Tora Bora." I highly recommend watching it. Co-director Wazhmah Osman returns to her home in Afghanistan to piece together the life that was torn apart by the 1979 Soviet invasion.

I find it sad that sometimes when talking to people I soon realize how little they know about what happened in the 1980s and 1990s in Afghanistan and how simplified their understanding of these complicated and complex geopolitical events are. I hope historians and teachers will make an effort to ensure that our next generation of young men and women are more knowledgeable about the true nature of these past conflicts so they do not see everything as black and white, and/or blame all the problems of the world on the 1.6 billion Muslim people. The vast majority of Muslims are no different than other ordinary people; they love peace, they love their family, they want a good education for their children, they work hard and don't want to be singled out when extremists hijack their religion to kill innocent people. I also need to tell the hypocritical politicians who spread fear, bigotry and division that no matter how hard you try, you will fail, because I have faith and hope in our next generation of young men and women. The United States is one of the best countries in the world. As a Muslim American, I would do everything in my power to defend this country and know that my children are very lucky and proud to live in this amazing country and call themselves Americans.

I started to write this memoir during the United States Presidential election campaign in 2016. Donald Trump and Hillary Clinton, the two most unpopular presidential candidates, became the nominees of their political parties to run for the office of the President of the United States. Since my personal life had been impacted by politics, wars and conflicts, I have always been interested in following political events around the world, although I never joined a political movement or party. In fact, I consider myself as a centrist, and do believe that Republicans, Democrats and

Independents all love this country but have different approaches and ideas on how to address socioeconomic and political issues that impact our lives.

What really shocked me is how Donald Trump, an eccentric, egomaniac, and narcissistic individual with clear racist tendencies managed to win the Republican Primaries and then the general election to become the 45th President of this great country. Donald Trump started his presidential campaign by insulting immigrants and Mexicans by calling them rapists and criminals. He insulted a respected federal judge who was assigned to handle one of the cases alleging fraud against him, the so called "Trump University," because the judge was of Hispanic heritage. He considers the media as the enemy of the nation and continues to call journalists dishonest and disgusting. As an opportunistic and unstable person, he called for a ban on all Muslims from entering the United States of America. He mocked a disabled journalist, continued to demean women by making obscene comments about their looks and intellects. He bragged on tape that he could do anything to any woman, even grabbing them by their genitals because he was rich and powerful.

What I found even more shocking: that his insulting and sexually predatory comments about women were viewed by some of his supporters as acceptable "locker room talk."

Really?

In my humble opinion, his insulting comments caught on tape exposed his true character, and I am still shocked that as a nation people voted for someone like him to hold the highest office in the land. I did hear comments from some of my friends who voted for him that they had other reasons to vote for him. They wanted to make sure that Hillary Clinton did not get elected, that the Supreme Court vacancy would be filled by a conservative judge, that they were tired of typical politicians who had disappointed them in the past, and that they wanted change.

But how about the simple argument that Mr. Trump with his lack of experience in foreign policy, his eccentric views about almost every topic, his racist tendencies, and juvenile daily tweeting, and continuously making up untrue conspiracy theories? For years he falsely claimed that first African American President of the Unites States was not born in America.

Does character matter anymore, especially when someone is running for the highest office of the Nation?

Despite all of his craziness, racist tendencies, bigotry and instability, decent American people voted to elect him as the 45th President of the United States. He did lose the popular vote to his rival by 3 million votes, but he still managed to become the President. He falsely claimed without any evidence that 3 million illegal immigrants voted in the presidential elections. He continued to praise Vladimir Putin, despite many questions about Russia's involvement in helping Donald Trump win the elections. What really saddens me is that I know some of the people who voted for him. They are very honorable, decent people and some are my good friends. Most other prominent republican politicians, who throughout the presidential campaign were very critical of Donald Trump, at the end supported him. He is now representing the brand of the Republican Party. History will hopefully judge the political hypocrisy of those who aligned themselves with a narcissistic person who continues to brag about how smart he is because his uncle, John Trump, had been a professor at the Massachusetts Institute of Technology. Of course, according to Physics Today, the MIT professor's cerebral, collaborative approach to his work *"stands in striking contrast to his nephew's brash presidential campaign."*

In his first week in office, President Trump signed a number of controversial Executive Orders. One of the orders he signed was to ban Muslims from several countries from entering the United States. He also decided to severally limit Muslim refugees, mainly from the war-torn country of Syria, to come to the United States. President Trump either does not know or just does not care that Syrian refugees are the first victims of terrorists and a ruthless dictator, Bashar Al Assad, who used chemical weapons on innocent civilians. Mr. Trump may not know that most terrorist events that happened in the United States are either committed by American-born citizens or people who were already legally living in the United States, or by people from "friendly" Arab countries such as Saudi Arabia, which was not on his list of banned countries. I am still hopeful that President Trump will surround himself with people who can change his eccentric views about the world, women, Muslims, immigrants and other minorities and create a society that is not based on hate and fear, but instead based on tolerance, peace, and a belief that the diversity in America is a unique asset and not a threat. I also hope that his favorable views about dictators, and ruthless leaders such as Vladimir Putin, Bashar Al Assad, General El-Sisi, President Erdogan, and others will change. I still have faith in the American people and firmly believe that tolerance, courage, and respect for one another will defeat fear.

Looking at the current conflicts in Syria, Iraq, Egypt, Yemen, Libya, Nigeria, and many other unlucky countries, I feel the same pain for their innocent civilians that I feel for my people.

Young lives are lost.

Young generations are lost.

Why?

I am worried that with every new conflict we have a tendency to forget about past conflicts and tragedies and don't learn from them. I often wonder how much people know about the Soviet Union invasion of Afghanistan, and especially how much they know about the atrocities that the Soviets have committed in my homeland.

By writing this book, I am hoping that people learn that Afghanistan has not always been in the headlines because of Taliban cruelty, suicide bombings, or terrorist activities. Prior to the invasion of Afghanistan by the Soviet Union, my beautiful and beloved homeland had been a peaceful, tolerant, and moderate Islamic country.

What the Soviets and their allies did in Afghanistan is a tragedy of momentous proportions, a catalyst for most of the subsequent tragedies, wars, and conflicts that are still going on. I also hope that other powerful countries, such as the United States, when getting involved in conflicts similar to Afghanistan, should have a long term, thoughtful, and responsible post-war policy. All of the major powers involved in the Afghan conflicts and what happened after the defeat of the Soviet Union are directly responsible for the miseries and tragedies that continue to haunt not only the poor Afghan people but also the rest of the world.

The United States with its powerful armed forces is able to win wars, but I would like to submit that what they do after winning a war is even more important. During the Iraq war, I remember vividly an interview with General David Petraeus who, despite some personal mistakes, is considered as one of the most intellectual minds in the United States military. He was assigned as the first commander of the Multi-National Security Transition team in Iraq. In one of his interviews, a prominent journalist asked him whether or not he needed more soldiers. I do not remember his response verbatim, but here is a summary of what I remember about the response he gave:

What are needed in Iraq are not more soldiers, but more civil servants who understand their culture, the Iraqi people, religious differences, local traditions, and the language. Civil servants who can build a stable institution and help rebuild destroyed infrastructures, such as roads and bridges, schools and hospitals etc. Young and brave 20-year-old American soldiers are risking their lives, but they are not trained for what to do after winning the war.

Unfortunately, powerful American politicians made the same mistake in Iraq as they did in Afghanistan after the defeat of the Soviet Union. I know it is costly to do what General Petraeus suggested. But looking at what is going on right now, I firmly believe that the cost of a well-thought-out, post-war plan and careful policy is significantly less expensive, in terms of financial and human cost, than just leaving and creating a void that would lead to chaos, civil wars and extremist groups to flourish and threaten the entire world.

Recently President Trump, who is one of the least knowledgeable American Presidents regarding how to deal with the global challenges America is facing, proposed to significantly increase spending for the United States military, while slashing the budgets of other institutions such as the State Department, that would need more civil servants to help with stabilizing countries such as Iraq after the war. I am still hopeful that people around President Trump help him by clearly explaining the foreign policy mistakes of the past, and provide him with the guidance needed to have a more responsible and balanced foreign policy.

Photos

My passport ID photo - last year of high school -1981

Dad when he was a Governor in Afghanistan

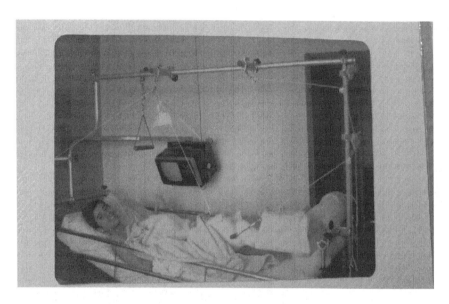

After my first surgery in El Paso Texas – 1978

**Our road trip from El Paso to Las Vegas
after my surgeries -1978**

My Ph.D. Defense - University of Paris XII - 1990

My Ph.D. Defense Committee - University of Paris XII -1990

Celebrating my Ph.D. Defense -1990

Ahmad Ansari

65529718R00128

Made in the USA
Middletown, DE
28 February 2018